Love Ben Toney
+ family
xx.

NORFOLK DIALECT
and its Friends

NORFOLK DIALECT AND ITS FRIENDS

Ten years
of FOND memories
recalled
by Robin Limmer

JOHN NICKALLS PUBLICATIONS

First published 2009
Copyright © Robin Limmer 2009

All rights reserved. No part of this publication may be reproduced in any form, or by any means, without the prior consent of the author.

ISBN 978 1 904136 29 3

Published by John Nickalls Publications
Oak Farm Bungalow, Sawyers Lane, Suton,
Wymondham, Norfolk NR18 9SH

Printed by The Complete Product Company Limited
Unit 20a, Diss Business Park, Hopper Way, Sandy Lane,
Diss, Norfolk IP22 4GT

CONTENTS

***The Merry Mawkin* Miscellany**

Foreword by Keith Skipper

IT WAS MY PLEASURE to follow his flashing hoe, banish renegade weeds and reduce any clumps he might have missed to a single beet plant. My heart sank, my back ached and my eyes misted over as he turned at the end to start yet another chopping-out marathon.

Then, just as I was losing the will to live, he'd draw out an old pocket watch, scan the skies and trundle towards me to exclaim: "Blarst, boy, dunt time floy out here!"

The signal for blessed relief.

Those words often came back to taunt me during a highly undistinguished spell as an apprentice son of the soil. I heard them again as FOND foreman Robin Limmer hailed completion of ten packed acres in the massive field of dialect appreciation.

Can it really be a decade since we tilled the ground, sowed the seeds and called for willing workers to tend the rows?

Well, it's been a back-breaking exercise at times, with far too many weeds of apathy and derision to clear away. But, to quote another good old Norfolk boy from my youth, "Reckun we're a'gittin' there!"

Friends of Norfolk Dialect are making a difference. It was my honour to lead them into battle against radio and television productions making a dog's breakfast of geography, local pride and artistic accuracy with Mummerzet abominations. (The malady lingers on.)

An important battle, but not the only one. We must do more to restore natural pride in 'torkin' proper' in local schools and communities at large. It shouldn't be just an amusing novelty to hear dialect words and phrases employed, more a regular feature of our cultural and social life.

In praising those who have worked overtime to spread the right words since the raising of our official standard in 1999, I mourn the loss of dear friends like Terry Davy and Tony Clarke. Best tribute we can pay them is to keep on complaining, cajoling, campaigning, canvassing and convincing.

I applaud old newspaper colleague Robin Limmer for the way he has pulled together colourful threads of the FOND saga so far. This anniversary tapestry gives extra shine to those words I wrote in my diary on Sunday, October 3rd, 1999, after a momentous meeting at Yaxham:

> "A day for celebration, a day I hope future generations will salute with gratitude."

Now it's time to tackle fresh rows up and down that Norfolk field. More long rows leading eventually to the headlands of hope.

Keith Skipper
Cromer, 2009

Introduction

MENTION YOU'RE A JOURNALIST today and it won't always impress, but if you're in Norfolk or north Suffolk and say you worked on the *Eastern Daily Press*, invariably interest is shown and affection expressed for the UK's leading regional morning newspaper.

I was privileged to be with the *EDP* for 37 years and offers from Fleet Street, Manchester and even Buenos Aires did not tempt me from my home county. Often colleagues who left Norwich for London or elsewhere eventually returned to Norfolk, never to stray again, although, of course, others became household names having learned their craft to perfection in East Anglia.

Across the editorial room on the *EDP* sports desk in those early days was a young journalist called Keith Skipper. By the time I retired in 1992 he himself was a household name through his *Dinnertime Show* on BBC Radio Norfolk and I joined him there on occasions.

Seventeen years later, Keith, MBE and a Deputy Lieutenant of the county, has become a Norfolk icon like many of the people he has written about in his books, now totalling well over 30, and I am grateful to him for allowing me to quote freely from them and, indeed, for writing the foreword to this book about Friends of Norfolk Dialect, of which he was founder-chairman.

I am indebted to Peter Franzen who, as editor of the *Eastern Daily Press*, permitted me to delve into the massive files of cuttings and pictures at Prospect House, and to librarian Rosemary Dixon who has been indispensable in searching for, and finding, some 40 staff pictures for this book.

Thanks also to Lyn McKinney, colleagues at Radio Norfolk and BBC East and to all the contributors I've contacted – from the

Seychelles to Sheringham, Catalonia to Cromer and France to Framingham Pigot.

Special thanks to my successor as editor of *The Merry Mawkin*, Ashley Gray, for his sterling work on the design of this volume, to the publisher, John Nickalls, and to my wife Shelagh for always being there when the computer misbehaved.

Robin Limmer
Denton, 2009

CHAPTER 1

All the King's Men

WHEN THE BBC FILM *All the King's Men* was screened in November 1999, it provided the newly-formed Friends of Norfolk Dialect with perfectly-timed evidence.

For it confirmed what many of us born in the county had known for years – that when the Norfolk accent is attempted by the broadcasting media, more often than not the result is a plethora of Mummerzet, a vaguely rural concoction which would probably be unrecognisable in any region of England.

The birth of FOND took place, as you would expect, in the very heart of Norfolk, while its conception had been achieved in almost all corners of the county and the Waveney Valley.

PICTURE: JEAN EAGLEN

How it all began: Yaxham Village Hall, Sunday, October 3, 1999. Chairman Keith Skipper and Peter Brooks on stage at the inaugural meeting of FOND.

Keith Skipper (left), champion of all things Norfolk, and Peter Trudgill, professor of English Linguistics. Keith was FOND's first chairman and Peter its president.

It was on the afternoon of Sunday, October 3, 1999, at Yaxham, near Dereham – just about as close to the centre of Norfolk as it's possible to get – that some 50 people gathered in the Village Hall to agree a constitution, set up an organising committee and decide on future action in which FOND would strive to preserve the unique sound and character of the county's dialect.

And then, as if to order, a few weeks later, *All the King's Men* marched on to our TV screens on Remembrance Sunday, November 14. Starring David Jason, Maggie Smith and David Troughton, the feature-length First World War drama was based on the story of the 1/5th (Territorial) Battalion of the Norfolk Regiment, which included men from King George V's estate at Sandringham House.

The battalion suffered heavy losses in action at Gallipoli on August 12, 1915, and a myth grew up that the unit had advanced into a mist and simply disappeared. Later a royal investigator was sent to try to establish the truth about the unit's fate and it was claimed, controversially, that the soldiers were taken prisoner by the Turkish Army and massacred.

David Jason won Best Actor in the TV Quick Awards for his

performance in the film, which was generally well received, but, in Norfolk, particularly in FOND, there was scathing criticism of the cast's attempts at depicting the county's accent.

FOND's founder-chairman, entertainer, broadcaster and author Keith Skipper wrote at the time: "Perfect timing, eh? FOND flexes its muscles as another big-name television production makes a mockery of the Norfolk tongue.

"*All the King's Men* from Sandringham assembled proudly, then marched into the same old murky Mummerzet waters.

"Perhaps BBC Television drama chiefs muttered hopes that such linguistic liberties did not spoil your enjoyment of this high-class programme too much.

"But obvious qualities on a major stage merely emphasised a blatant lack of authenticity when it came to 'local' voices. We have heard them all before. Countless times. Along predictable excuses about the Norfolk sound being so difficult to capture and not enough professional actors and actresses able to give it a reasonable go. And to think they have the cheek to include 'dialect coach' in the credits!"

Keith continued: "The over-sensitive dialect lobby took a bow in the *Eastern Daily Press* letters columns as correspondents shared their views on the production. Over-sensitive? I would prefer to call us genuinely concerned about the way Norfolk people are portrayed to national and international audiences on television, radio and stage.

"If we don't show concern, who will? And would it be too much of an exaggeration to suggest many supporters have joined FOND in the express hope of signalling an end to this long-running saga of counterfeit accents?"

When Keith Skipper was a full-time broadcaster with BBC Radio Norfolk, and increasingly frustrated by the Mummerzet treatment from all areas of the national media, he sent cassettes of Norfolk voices to various television and radio departments. "There were no acknowledgments, no follow-up inquiries, no acceptance that there were any wrongs to put right," he said. "Apathy or arrogance? Probably a mixture of the two.

"Norfolk's cussed streak remains the best hope of banishing the galling habit of lumping country dialects together and stirring them up in one big rustic pot. FOND vows to lead the fight to put individual

FOND's first secretary, Tony Clarke...

character and respect for truly local tradition at the centre of all stages."

FOND's first secretary was Tony Clarke who, although living at Beccles, just across the border, had a fine Norfolk pedigree. Indeed, as the smock-clad yokel the Boy Jimma, he was for many years one of the stars of Keith Skipper's Press Gang band of local entertainers which appeared in village halls throughout the county and raised some £20,000 for the *EDP* 'We Care' charity and thousands for local causes.

Sadly, after a three-year battle with cancer, Tony died in November, 2008. Following three years as secretary of FOND, he had been elected vice-chairman at the AGM in the autumn of 2002 and became chairman in 2005, standing down in 2006 because of increasing ill-health.

From January, 2000, Tony produced and wrote the script for an annual pantomime at North Elmham Memorial Institute which became one of the highlights of the FOND social year, always attracting a near-capacity audience irrespective of the wintry weather outside.

His last production was in January, 2008, the year of his death, and even in his final months he was compiling a collection of the scripts used over the previous nine years for possible future use.

Soon after the screening of *All the King's Men*, Tony, in a letter to the *EDP* in November, 1999, stated: "Norfolk seems to be an increasingly fertile environment for TV dramas, which is hardly surprising given the colourful history of our once-remote and fiercely independent fiefdom.

...and as the Boy Jimma. Tony Clarke was one of the stars of Keith Skipper's Press Gang, and the producer and scriptwriter of FOND's annual pantomime.

"However, it was a cause of great disappointment to us that *All the King's Men* could not avoid the trap into which so many previous TV productions have fallen, which is to depict proud Norfolk people as yokels, speaking with a vaguely rural accent which would probably be totally unrecognisable in any region of England.

"For all I know, the inhabitants of other English counties may also have come to the conclusion that programme-makers, who in all other respects search diligently for authenticity and accuracy when producing drama-documentaries, seem to think that when they need to portray country people any old lingo will do. The result is we all sound like village idiots.

"Friends of Norfolk Dialect exists to conserve the authentic voice of Norfolk. It already has among its membership people with considerable expertise in their subject, and the amazing rate at which that membership is increasing indicates huge potential support for our objectives.

"Is it too fanciful to speculate that one day there may be a Department of Dialect at the University of East Anglia?"

Certainly, as Tony mentioned, FOND's membership includes great expertise – not least that of its president, Norwich-born Professor Peter Trudgill, until retirement in 2005 chair of English Linguistics at the University of Fribourg, Switzerland.

After jetting in from Switzerland, Professor Trudgill said at FOND's first social gathering – a 'FOND-dew' – at Yaxham Village Hall in March, 2000, that the society's formation marked a trend that was happening worldwide.

Dick Squittington, produced by Tony Clarke (left, in front of stage) and starring a cast of 'volunteers' from a packed house at North Elmham Memorial Institute in January, 2008. It was Tony's last pantomime. He died ten months later.

"It is part of the wider development to counteract cultural homogenisation. It is important to stand up for local identity and local culture. I would like to see more respect for the Norfolk dialect and Norfolk accent and not just from local residents," he said.

"I would like to see the BBC respect it more when they try to feature it on television and see it get more respect around the country."

Thus, Friends of Norfolk Dialect was blessed with strong leadership from the start, with Keith Skipper, Peter Trudgill and Tony Clarke capably heading a very talented committee.

I would venture to say that FOND had – still has – two jewels in its crown: a double-diamond, which, like the old beer ad, works wonders.

For here was Keith, the champion of all things Norfolk, with long experience in journalism, broadcasting, authorship and entertaining, with Peter, a professor of linguistics, Norfolk-born but based in Switzerland and world-renowned in this field, giving the new organisation authority and respect far beyond the boundaries of the county.

As 1999 drew to a close, all seemed set fair for FOND. Members were looking forward to the appearance, early in the new year, of its first newsletter which would galvanise kindred spirits and help spread the word throughout the county and far beyond. However, tragedy was about to intervene…

CHAPTER 2

Tragedy

IT WAS JOHN AUSTRIN, of Stalham, who thought up the name that was to find a place in the county's archives. He pointed out that FOND is a perfect description of how enthusiasts feel about their dialect. "I was delighted when my idea was adopted," he said.

Meanwhile, *Eastern Daily Press* cartoonist Tony Hall produced a striking design featuring a scarecrow, or mawkin as it is known in Norfolk, and this became not only the FOND permanent logo but also provided the basis for the alliterative title of our newsletter, *The Merry Mawkin*.

By December, 1999, all was going well in preparation for a bumper launch in mid-January of the first edition of *The Merry Mawkin*.

Its editor was the Dereham publisher Terry Davy, who had played a key role in setting up FOND and had taken on the editorship with relish, his impressive grasp of all the latest technology and a reputation as an outstanding local publisher making him a natural choice for the post. Then tragically, a few days before Christmas, Terry died of a heart attack at the early age of fifty-nine.

Obviously, this sad loss threw a host of FOND hopes into disarray. However, to the rescue came another well-known figure on the local publishing scene, Jim Baldwin of Fakenham, stepping in as 'emergency editor', a task he accepted out of respect for Terry's memory as well as providing a mark of his own backing for our precious vernacular.

The FOND logo designed by EDP cartoonist Tony Hall.

Tony Hall, EDP cartoonist.

A few weeks later Jim produced the very first edition of the *Mawkin*, of necessity a much smaller publication than the one Terry had planned, but the four A5 pages played a valuable part in keeping the new organisation's members in touch.

In addition to the coverage of the death of its editor, Edition 1 included rallying articles by president Professor Peter Trudgill and chairman Keith Skipper, together with the list of officers, forthcoming fixtures for the Press Gang concerts and, most important, the future date and details of the first FOND-dew, on March 19th at Yaxham Village Hall.

And now a search began... Four days before the Yaxham FOND-dew, Keith wrote in his weekly *EDP* column, 'Skipper's Byways': "FOND is anxious to find someone to take on the role of newsletter editor following the untimely death of Terry Davy just before Christmas. An 'emergency' edition came out recently, but it is hoped future copies of *The Merry Mawkin* will be much bigger and bolder.

"The newsletter will play an important part as a platform for news and views in the battle to keep our dialect alive. A grasp of the latest technology is essential for the post, while some experience in journalism would be useful.

"If you feel you have what it takes to prepare two or three editions of the FOND newsletter a year, please bring your credentials to Yaxham on Sunday or drop me a line."

Keith repeated his appeal at the FOND-dew, but to no immediate avail.

I had an uncomfortable feeling that I might be approached (journalist with the *EDP* for 37 years, etc) if no one else put his/her head above the parapet. Already involved in the Waveney Valley with the *Three Rivers Talking Newspaper for the Blind* and with several other commitments, I decided that if I were asked I would make my excuses and... ...well no, not leave, but help in other ways.

And indeed it came to pass... a phone call a few weeks later from FOND secretary Tony Clarke (incidentally, an old *EDP* colleague of mine). A very understanding Tony took 'no' for an answer, but not before he'd persuaded me to put my name down for election to the committee.

It was at this point that another *EDP* colleague came to the rescue. Martin Kirby, the newspaper's deputy editor, was already FOND's vice-chairman and was obviously an ideal choice to take over the editorship of *The Merry Mawkin*.

And so in the summer of 2000, tripled in size to twelve pages, Edition 2 of *The Merry Mawkin* went out to FOND's 200 or so members (increasing by the week). Martin had done a splendid job. 'Looking ahead with Fondness', was the headline of the lead story written by chairman Keith, while another of Norfolk's best-known sons, Sid Kipper, contributed what was to prove the first of many brilliant dialect-laden side-splitting articles to entertain *Mawkin* readers for years to come.

Comedian Sid, for long familiar in his home county through regular appearances on Keith's *Dinnertime Show* on BBC Radio Norfolk and in village halls throughout the region, is Norfolk's ambassador on the entertainment front the length and breadth of Britain, and no one has brought our dialect before the rest of the country more since the days of the Singing Postman, Allan Smethurst, in the 1960s when his *Hev Yew Gotta Loight, Boy?* hit the national charts.

This is how Keith described Sid Kipper in his *EDP* column in October 2001: "The self-styled Norfolk megastar combines writing, singing and story-telling in such seamless fashion it is difficult to know where to fit him on the entertainment menu.

"Performances on stage and in print mark him as our leading cultural ambassador, failing lamentably to live up to his own maxim that a pleasure shared is a pleasure halved. His latest literary opus, *Cod Pieces* (in crispy banter), filleted to perfection with the help of alter ego Chris Sugden, can only enhance a growing reputation for top-class 'squilture.'

"Yes, it is necessary to invent a new word to describe this potent mixture of squit and culture. Sid takes it all over the country, and occasionally abroad, to show Norfolk is way ahead of the field in lateral thinking.

"*Cod Pieces* is a tasty collection of short stories and tall tales from the small village of St Just-near-Trunch. Thorough scrutiny of a map of Norfolk to find this tiny parish would leave the searcher none the wiser."

Elsewhere in Edition 2 of the *Mawkin*, there were articles by the *EDP's* former London editor, Maurice Woods, who for many years wrote the highly-respected and amusing 'Harbert's News from Dumpton' broad Norfolk column in the Norwich Mercury Series of weekly newspapers.

Other contributions included one from The Gal Liza (Elizabeth Austrin), a treasured member of Keith's Press Gang, the *EDP's* then new dialect correspondent, upholding the tradition set by the legendary Norfolk dialect character The Boy John, portrayed by Sidney Grapes, of Potter Heigham.

All seemed set for a bright future for *The Merry Mawkin* now that, at last, a new editor had been appointed and had launched his own first edition.

Alas, it was a short-lived reign and, before the next edition could be published, yet another new editor would have to be found.

CHAPTER 3

Editor emigrates!

FOND WAS A YEAR OLD in October, 2000, celebrated on the 29th at its AGM in Yaxham Village Hall when chairman Keith Skipper reported an eventful and successful 12 months. Equally glowing reports came from secretary Tony Clarke, treasurer Janet Woodhouse and membership secretary Brenda Bizzell.

Officers and committee were re-elected en-bloc and two additional committee members were appointed, Rita-Ann Kirk and myself. A highly entertaining but, of necessity, non-political talk was given by the Conservative MP for Mid-Norfolk, Keith Simpson, Norfolk-born and City of Norwich School old boy.

A few weeks later, I attended my first FOND committee meeting, travelling from the Waveney Valley with Tony Clarke to the Cromer home of Keith Skipper and his wife, Diane.

And then came some surprise and startling news. Chairman Keith read a letter of resignation from Martin Kirby, our vice-chairman and the editor of *The Merry Mawkin.*

Martin Kirby, newly-appointed editor of The Merry Mawkin, emigrated to Spain in 2001.

No Going Back was not only the title of Martin's book, relating to the Kirby family's move to Catalonia, but also that of the Channel 4 TV series.

He and his young family were emigrating in the new year to Spain where he planned to run an organic farm in Catalonia and to write. It meant, of course, that Martin, a long-serving journalist with the *Eastern Daily Press* and its associated newspapers, would resign as *EDP* deputy editor.

> *The big move was to prove a successful one for the Kirby family and in the next nine years they were to establish a productive 10-acre farm, known as Mother's Garden, and were quickly accepted into the local community.*
>
> *Martin began writing a monthly column in the EDP, networked in the East Anglian Daily Times and the Yorkshire Post, and the family featured in the British Channel 4 television series, No Going Back.*
>
> *Moreover, Martin has written two books, No Going Back – Journey to Mother's Garden and a Norfolk-based novel, Count the Petals of the Moon Daisy, which was top of Jarrolds' best-seller charts in Norfolk for several months in 2008 and may be made into a film.*

An article Martin wrote from Catalonia for *The Merry Mawkin* in 2002 appears on Page 175.

Back to that committee meeting at Keith's in November 2000...

After Martin's resignation letter had been read, I found myself at the centre of attention when the subject of a new editor for *The Merry Mawkin* was discussed. This time there was no escape!

And so, early in 2001, I set out to produce my first *Merry Mawkin*, a unique situation in that each of the first three editions would have been produced by a different editor.

Before retiring from the *EDP* in 1992, I had worked through the revolutionary changes in news production in which reporters filed their stories on screen instead of on paper, and sub-editors like myself, instead of handling the news copy with the use of pen or pencil, now edited the news at a computer screen.

So now I was confronted with a desk-top publishing task of producing the third edition of FOND's newsletter, and with the help of my computer-literate wife Shelagh as technical adviser, the 12-page issue hit the streets of Norfolk and beyond in the spring of 2001.

In the front-page lead story, Keith stated that as Friends of Norfolk Dialect squared up to the challenges of a second year in operation, it was clear the honeymoon period was over – and the routine hard graft had started.

"Indeed, as FOND's voice grows louder, both in this county and beyond, agitation and aggression must be matched by achievement," he wrote. "It was right to put down proper roots, to set out specific aims in the name of conserving and recording our priceless linguistic and cultural heritage. Plenty of laughs along the way – and that will continue to be the case – but this is a serious campaign with long-term ambitions.

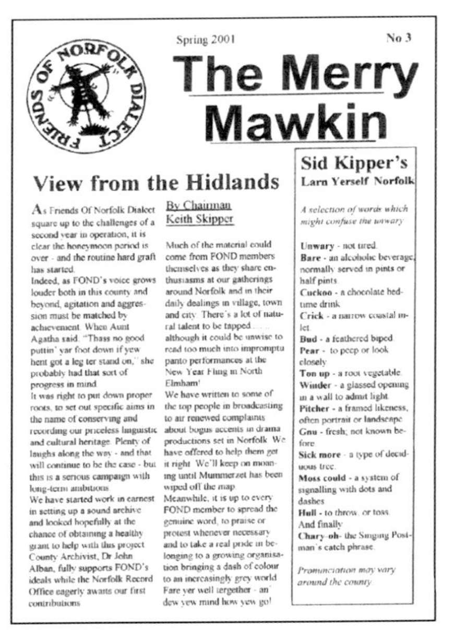

Spring 2001 No 3

FRIENDS OF NORFOLK DIALECT

The Merry Mawkin

View from the Hidlands

By Chairman Keith Skipper

As Friends Of Norfolk Dialect square up to the challenges of a second year in operation, it is clear the honeymoon period is over - and the routine hard graft has started.

Indeed, as FOND's voice grows louder both in this county and beyond, agitation and aggression must be matched by achievement. When Aunt Agatha said: "Thass no good puttin' yar foot down if yew hent got a leg ter stand on," she probably had that sort of progress in mind.

It was right to put down proper roots, to set out specific aims in the name of conserving and recording our priceless linguistic and cultural heritage. Plenty of laughs along the way - and that will continue to be the case - but this is a serious campaign with long-term ambitions.

We have started work in earnest in setting up a sound archive and looked hopefully at the chance of obtaining a healthy grant to help with this project. County Archivist, Dr John Alban, fully supports FOND's ideals while the Norfolk Record Office eagerly awaits our first contributions.

Much of the material could come from FOND members themselves as they share enthusiasms at our gatherings around Norfolk and in their daily dealings in village, town and city. There's a lot of natural talent to be tapped...... although it could be unwise to read too much into impromptu panto performances at the New Year Fling in North Elmham!

We have written to some of the top people in broadcasting to air renewed complaints about bogus accents in drama productions set in Norfolk. We have offered to help them get it right. We'll keep on moaning until Mummerzet has been wiped off the map.

Meanwhile, it is up to every FOND member to spread the genuine word, to praise or protest whenever necessary and to take a real pride in belonging to a growing organisation bringing a dash of colour to an increasingly grey world.

Fare yer well tergether - an' dew yew mind how yew go!

Sid Kipper's Larn Yerself Norfolk

A selection of words which might confuse the unwary

Unwary - not tired.
Bare - an alcoholic beverage, normally served in pints or half pints.
Cuckoo - a chocolate bedtime drink.
Crick - a narrow coastal inlet.
Bud - a feathered biped.
Pear - to peep or look closely.
Ton up - a root vegetable.
Winder - a glassed opening in a wall to admit light.
Pitcher - a framed likeness, often portrait or landscape.
Gnu - fresh; not known before.
Sick more - a type of deciduous tree.
Moss could - a system of signalling with dots and dashes.
Hull - to throw, or toss.
And finally
Chary-oh- the Singing Postman's catch phrase.

Pronunciation may vary around the county.

The Merry Mawkin: spring issue 2001.

"We have started work in earnest in setting up a sound archive and looked hopefully at the chance of obtaining a healthy grant to help with this project. County archivist Dr John Alban fully supports FOND's ideals, while the Norfolk Record Office eagerly awaits our first contributions."

Keith added: "We have written to some of the top people in broadcasting to air renewed complaints about bogus accents in drama productions set in Norfolk. We have offered to help them get it right. We'll keep on moaning until Mummerzet has been wiped off the map.

"Meanwhile, it is up to every FOND member to spread the genuine word, to praise or protest whenever necessary and to take a real pride in belonging to a growing organisation bringing a dash of colour to an increasingly grey world."

Elsewhere in Edition 3 were articles by two men who were destined to play crucial roles in the future of FOND – Peter Brooks and Colin Burleigh. Both were founder members and served on the committee from the beginning.

Peter, curator of Sheringham Museum and author of a number of local history books and others, would later become vice-chairman and then chairman from 2002–2005.

Colin, comedian stalwart of Keith's Press Gang, jazz musician and vocalist, film extra, sometime dialect coach and Jarrolds' Father Christmas, was elected FOND chairman in the autumn of 2006. As The Boy Colin, he has contributed a dialect article and a Norfolk quiz in each *Merry Mawkin* since 2001.

Another writer whose work was to become an important feature in the *Mawkin* – usually in the form of a 'centre-page spread' – was Ron Fiske, Norfolk antiquary and book-collector, with his long-running series 'The Norfolk Dialect: Guides to Reading and Research'.

Ron's learned articles, together with those of president Professor Peter Trudgill and Dr William Woods, director of the Dutch and Flemish Studies Centre in Norwich, provided *The Merry Mawkin* with an impressive supply of academia, contrasting nicely, on other pages, with broad Norfolk humour, news of FOND's work in preserving the dialect through recordings, schools visits and the website, plus local book reviews, members' letters and e-mails and, not least, Brenda Bizzell's 'Norfolk Wordsearch' puzzle.

And so, with a sigh of relief that my first *Mawkin* had, somehow, become a reality, I set about planning Edition 4. Publication would be in June, 2001, and now we could expand – from 12 pages to 20.

CHAPTER 4

Norfolk by Adoption

THE EIGHT EXTRA PAGES enabled me to begin a new series in *The Merry Mawkin* which I'd been thinking about for some time. Entitled 'Norfolk by Adoption', its contributors would be people who, though not Norfolk-born, had made their permanent home in the county.

Who should I ask? I looked no further than two of my ex-*EDP* colleagues, my good friends **Bruce Robinson** and **David Williams**.

Bruce, author, publisher, *EDP* features and leader writer and Peddars' Way authority, grew up in a marshland town in South Lincolnshire in the 1940s and 1950s. Norfolk, he wrote, represented a kind of Eden:

> It was a land of mystery and freedom, a foreign land on the other side of the old windblown landlocked estuary which divided the two counties.
>
> It promised sunshine and hills, forests and leafy glades – all in short supply amid our never-ending vistas of broad beans, cereals, beet and potatoes and, if we were energetic enough, the seaside.
>
> Most summer Sundays a gang of us would pack sandwiches, roll up our waterproofs, check our tyres and take off on our bikes. We travelled up to 100 miles a day, sometimes as far as Hunstanton, the other side of the Wash.
>
> Sun, good friends, dry Hovis sandwiches and bottles of Corona. Occasional showers, a beefy front wind, tyres encrusted with gravel and tar. The smell of the road. Magic!

In 1951, it all came to an end when the number of vehicles brought increasing discomfort to cyclists, the putrid air stank of fumes and Bruce and his friends decided to put an end to their jaunts.

Bruce Robinson: 'My particular road to Damascus was a quiet lane in Breckland, fringed by wide verges and tall plantations.'

Bruce continued:

Not until 1959 did Norfolk figure in my thoughts again, and that was because of another job on another newspaper, this time in Norwich (the *EDP*). But there was little opportunity to explore anywhere except Carrow Road and dozens of football grounds scattered the length and breadth of the country.

Even marriage (to a Norfolk gel) and a young family allowed only occasional glimpses of the county's charms, mainly gleaned from family picnics or chaotic outings to beach or forest. So I suppose it was not until 1973 that the real conversion came. Then another change of newspaper, still with the *EDP*, suddenly gave me the freedom to roam (in search of copy, of course) almost where I wished.

My particular road to Damascus was a quiet lane in Breckland, fringed by wide verges and tall plantations. The sky was a brilliant blue, like a Sisley painting, the yellow-flecked gorse was almost out, and a light covering of snow dusted the treetops.

I pulled the car over, sun-blinded and dazzled, and was converted in a thrice. Back in Norwich I rushed to Jarrolds and bought a copy of Rainbird Clarke's *In Breckland Wilds*. This was the real beginning of an ultimately deeply satisfying fascination for the county which has lasted for decades.

Countryside and archaeology, tales and secrets, villages and market towns, curiosities and characters, walks and forests and seashores...

And so every time we, as a family, pondered whether to move in search of another job, we talked it over and then asked, Well, where is there a better place to live? Bristol? Birmingham? London? Get a life! (as they say nowdays).

So after over 40 years as a grateful resident, and with a wife and four Norfolk-born sons to prove my allegiance, if anybody asks, "Where are you from?" I invariably reply, "From Norfolk. And originally from Lincolnshire." When the 50 years are up, I promise to drop the 'originally'.

The second 'Norfolk by Adoption' piece was by **David Williams**, friend and colleague on the *EDP* for many years, but sadly now no longer with us, who came from Yorkshire and first visited Norfolk in 1953, joining the *Eastern Evening News* as a sub-editor in 1959. He wrote:

It was at the WI Strawberry Fair that I was accepted as an adopted Norfolkman. This was some 20 years ago and my 'adopter' was a local farmer who was so fiercely indigenous he once tried unilaterally to declare UDI for the county, but had failed on some minor technicality.

David Williams: 'My heart is right here!'

He questioned me closely and heard that I had first begun my association with my adopted county in 1953. This was almost historical and he was impressed. My best mate in the Army was a Norfolk boy – well, almost. Norwich really. Hellesdon, in fact.

He got demobbed before me, so while I was still keeping the Red hordes at bay, Her Majesty agreed to give me a week off, so I headed for Norfolk. I was met at Norwich Thorpe by Glen, who had borrowed his father's BSA Bantam to transport me to Hellesdon. Suffice to say we arrived safely.

I saw a lot of Norfolk that week, including the Broads (a memorable photograph beside Roys lavatories at Wroxham), the coast and Norwich Cattle Market, where Glen's girlfriend's father ran the café in Bell Avenue.

And so I'm grateful that life dealt me the card that brought me to Norfolk permanently in 1959. I'm grateful that I was able to experience a Norwich so different from the one today – a bustling, friendly city, a bit grimier but none the worse for it, with a host of interesting shops, pubs and people.

I believe it's been all downhill since local government reorganisation in 1973, when we no longer had a borough and when the town clerk became a chief executive and other people were given long titles far in excess of their abilities.

So I joined the *Eastern Evening News* as a sub-editor after an interesting introduction to journalism in South Yorkshire. I enjoyed the civilised atmosphere of the old Norfolk News Company, despite the fact that traces of the old forelock touching still remained.

My first real confrontation with the Norfolk dialect was when, just as the *Pink 'Un* was winding down on my first Saturday afternoon, the phone rang and there was the clerk of the markets office intent on giving me the prices of the day. I couldn't understand enough to be sure of accuracy and I was a bit worried about his reference to 'flying pigs,' so I hastily handed over to a colleague!

Outsiders were in the minority then, but I felt less of one after one of our regular Saturday lunchtime visits to the long bar at the Royal Hotel. Alfred Jenner, who then had the title of editorial executive, was a regular attender. 'Yes,' he conceded, 'all the Yorkshiremen we have employed so far have been all right.'

I must have been in that category as I lasted for another 30-plus years.

After a short absence of three years away in Norway (operating Lapland treks for Norfolk folk) and then in the West Country, I planted my roots permanently in Norfolk.

We bought a smallholding in south Norfolk and had cows, goats, sheep and chickens, grew all our vegetables and worked round about 30 hours a day.

For two years I worked for a farmer friend during the day and helped produce the *Eastern Daily Press* at night. So I learned about life in rural Norfolk the hard way – but I enjoyed every minute of it.

And my children, of course, are Norfolk-born and proud of it. My younger daughter, at university in London at present, says she's coming home when her studies are over – to stay.

Home is where the heart is, so they say, and my heart is right here!

ADVENTURE OF A LIFETIME

David mentioned that he spent three years away in Norway operating Lapland treks. That was in the late 1960s. Thirty years later, in 2000, David and his wife Marion, who first met on one of these treks, invited nine friends to accompany them on a nostalgic expedition beyond the Arctic Circle through Norway, Sweden and Finland to the Russian border.

EDP colleague Bruce Robinson was one of these friends and I was another. Laptrek 2000 was the adventure of a lifetime. The eleven of us left south Norfolk in two long-wheelbase Land-Rovers on July 24 and by the time we returned three weeks later on August 14 we had travelled 4,453 miles, having camped every night in all weathers in three countries.

At North Cape (Nordkapp) we watched the midnight sun set and rise a few minutes later. On our return from the Russian border near Murmansk, beside the Barents Sea, we travelled south via the Norwegian mainland to Bergen, diverting to camp on the Lofoten Islands in transit.

CHAPTER 5

National limelight

AN ENCOURAGING GRANT of £3,889 for FOND from the National Lottery Fund made the lead story on the front page of Edition 4 of *The Merry Mawkin* in the autumn of 2001, and it brought our organisation into the national limelight.

Keith Skipper said the grant boosted FOND's crusade to preserve our dialect for future generations, paying for the first batch of recording equipment and archive fees as well as funding vital educational work.

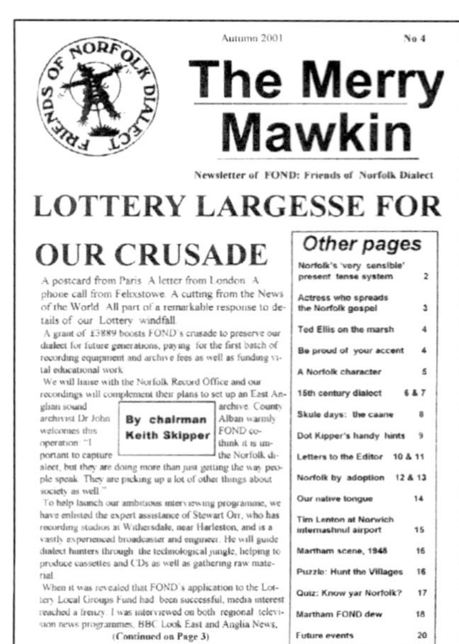

Autumn 2001 No 4

The Merry Mawkin

Newsletter of FOND: Friends of Norfolk Dialect

LOTTERY LARGESSE FOR OUR CRUSADE

By chairman Keith Skipper

A postcard from Paris. A letter from London. A phone call from Felixstowe. A cutting from the News of the World. All part of a remarkable response to details of our Lottery windfall.

A grant of £3889 boosts FOND's crusade to preserve our dialect for future generations, paying for the first batch of recording equipment and archive fees as well as funding vital educational work.

We will liaise with the Norfolk Record Office and our recordings will complement their plans to set up an East Anglian sound archive. County archivist Dr John Alban warmly welcomes this FOND co-operation: "I think it is important to capture the Norfolk dialect, but they are doing more than just getting the way people speak. They are picking up a lot of other things about society as well."

To help launch our ambitious interviewing programme, we have enlisted the expert assistance of Stewart Orr, who has recording studios at Withersdale, near Harleston, and is a vastly experienced broadcaster and engineer. He will guide dialect hunters through the technological jungle, helping to produce cassettes and CDs as well as gathering raw material.

When it was revealed that FOND's application to the Lottery Local Groups Fund had been successful, media interest reached a frenzy. I was interviewed on both regional television news programmes, BBC Look East and Anglia News,

(Continued on Page 3)

Other pages

Norfolk's 'very sensible' present tense system	2
Actress who spreads the Norfolk gospel	3
Ted Ellis on the marsh	4
Be proud of your accent	4
A Norfolk character	5
15th century dialect	6 & 7
Skule days: the caane	8
Dot Kipper's handy hints	9
Letters to the Editor	10 & 11
Norfolk by adoption	12 & 13
Our native tongue	14
Tim Lenton at Norwich internashnul airport	15
Martham scene, 1948	16
Puzzle: Hunt the Villages	16
Quiz: Know yar Norfolk?	17
Martham FOND dew	18
Future events	20

The Merry Mawkin: autumn issue 2001.

"We will liaise with the Norfolk Record Office and our recordings will complement their plans to set up an East Anglian sound archive. County archivist Dr John Alban, warmly welcoming this FOND co-operation, said: 'I think it is important to capture the Norfolk dialect, but they are doing more than just getting the way people speak. They are picking up a lot of other things about society as well'.

"To help launch our ambitious interviewing programme, we have enlisted the expert assistance of Stewart Orr, who has recording studios at

Withersdale, near Harleston, and is a vastly experienced broadcaster and engineer. He will guide dialect hunters through the technological jungle, helping to produce cassettes and CDs as well as gathering raw material.

"When it was revealed that FOND's application to the Lottery Local Groups Fund had been successful, media interest reached a frenzy. I was interviewed on both regional television news programmes, BBC *Look East* and Anglia News, while radio chats included spots on Radio 4 *Today* and the BBC World Service. National newspapers and magazines joined the fray – and a mention alongside less cultural pursuits in the *News of the World*!"

Dr John Alban, county archivist: 'It is important to capture the Norfolk dialect.'

Keith added that FOND membership had moved well past the 220 mark. "Calls from all over the country and a hefty postbag, including a postcard from a Norfolk exile in Paris and a letter from a radio producer in London, underline the bonus of such widespread publicity.

"Now it's on with the mardling for posterity – which doesn't mean sitting on our backsides!"

CHAPTER 6

A real Norfolk actress

JUST NOW AND AGAIN, it is possible to listen to a play on national radio and find that the genuine Norfolk accent is being delivered. For instance, it happens occasionally on BBC Radio 4 when FOND member **Patience Tomlinson** is in the cast.

Patience Tomlinson: 'Proud to be a member of FOND.'

For Patience was born at Brancaster, where her father was rector. She lives and works in London, but in the autumn of 2000 she put authentic Norfolk on the national stage when she read some of Mary Mann's harrowing Victorian stories on Radio 4.

She told *The Merry Mawkin* at the time: "Let us hope this radio series heralds the start of a more enlightened era when it comes to the Norfolk tongue," pledging support for FOND and its growing band of members.

And so, Patience Tomlinson wrote in the *Mawkin's* autumn edition of 2001, under the heading:

Actress spreads the Norfolk gospel

Isn't it funny how one thing leads to another? Last autumn I read some of Mary Mann's Tales from *Victorian Norfolk* on BBC Radio 4. A real treat for me to be given five whole stories to read and to be able to use my Norfolk dialect, which hadn't had much of a look in on radio lately.

Then Keith Skipper got in touch and we had a bit of a mardle on Radio Norfolk. Then I was asked to be in a play, based in Norwich, called *Promises to Keep*, by Vivienne Allen. The great thing about it was that nearly every one of the actors was Norfolk-born and bred.

If you heard it, I think (and hope) you'll agree it was a refreshing change from the usual Mummerzet that's supposed to pass for Norfolk. Christopher James spent his childhood in Sedgeford, just down the road from Docking where I was living. He played the lead, Martin, and very good he was too.

It was lovely and very rare to meet a whole Norfolk cast. I hope plenty of people were listening and noticed how distinct and unlike Mummerzet our dialect is. May it never die out! Thanks to FOND, there's a pretty strong chance it never will.

The sound and the rhythm, the unique words and special humour must be preserved and passed on for future generations, not just in books but as a living, breathing language.

Who would ever make sense of Mary Mann's wonderful stories in years to come otherwise? I am very proud to be a member of FOND and if it wasn't for Mary Mann I might never have heard about it.

Thass a rum ole, dew, int it? Cheeriooo!

In September, 2009, Patience added: I have written a one-woman play about the life and work of Mary Mann called A Tale That is Told, *which I perform in venues around East Anglia and further afield.*

Susan Yaxley of the Larks Press came to a performance in Mary Mann's home village of Shropham, near Attleborough, on which the Dulditch stories are based. Larks Press is republishing the best of Mann's 39 out-of-print novels and a complete collection of her Dulditch short stories, which are superb – especially for Norfolk dialect enthusiasts.

Astray in Arcady, *first published in 1910, about a London authoress visiting a Norfolk village, will be out in time for Christmas. A very good read! Further details: www.booksatlarkspress.co.uk.*

CHAPTER 7

Norfolk and Suffolk dialect similarities

I MENTIONED EARLIER that our president, **Professor Peter Trudgill**, wrote an article on dialect in each edition of *The Merry Mawkin*. In Edition 5, winter 2001, his subject was 'The Place of Norfolk among English dialects'.

After describing how the traditional English dialects of Britain are divided into two major geographical sub-groups, those of the North and those of the South, he went on to discuss the similarities between the Norfolk and Suffolk vernaculars:

> The boundary between Norfolk and Suffolk is less significant, of course, since they are both of the East Anglian area, and the dialects are very similar.
>
> Nevertheless, there are plenty of differences between the two. For example, splinters are called *shivers* in Norfolk, *slivers* in Suffolk. A snail is known as a *dodman* in Norfolk, a *hodmedod* in Suffolk. And the term *left-couch*, left-handed, is confined to Norfolk.
>
> The dialect boundary between Norfolk and Suffolk coincides mostly with the county boundary and thus the line of the Little Ouse and the Waveney.
>
> Unlike in the Old English period, however – no doubt as a result of the decline of importance of the Waveney as a barrier – much of north-eastern Suffolk is basically Norfolk rather than Suffolk-speaking.
>
> Beccles, Bungay and Lowestoft are certainly Norfolk-

speaking, and probably also places as far south in Suffolk as Halesworth and Southwold. These are places which 'look to' Norwich (and where people mostly support Norwich City rather than Ipswich Town) and the location of the dialect boundary reflects the relative historical influence of Norwich and Ipswich as urban centres.

The Norfolk dialect area is, of course, not uniform either. There are differences between the north-east, north-west, south-west and south-east of the area.

Gorse is known as *whinbush* in western Norfolk, but *furbish* or *furrabush* in the east. A mould-board on a plough is called a *plat* in north Norfolk, but a *breast* in the south.

And the urban dialects of Norwich, King's Lynn, Yarmouth/Gorleston and Lowestoft all have their own distinctive characteristics.

Elsewhere in the winter, 2001, edition of the *Mawkin* – now increased to 24 pages, the largest so far – was a book review linked with this subject of dialect in the two counties. There are, it stated, dialect words used indigenously in the Beccles area and to ensure that these were not lost, a booklet had been published locally which not only listed the words but recorded how they were used.

Beccles Talk 2001: A Speech Odyssey was written by Anne Frith, Dorothy Smith and Anne Bauers. "Here are recorded," said the authors, "some of those words, phrases and grammatical differences which could be heard in Beccles Market Place before the Second World War, those which could still be heard in Beccles Precinct at the very end of the 20th century and those dialect words which are recognised and/or used by some primary school-aged children in Beccles today."

These two gems from the book will appeal to everyone in the two counties north and south of the Waveney:

An old man described a spell of bad weather thus: "That blew, that snew, that friz and then that thew".

And in the double-negative department was recalled the remark by a Becclesian in 1937:

"Coo, that wholly rain las' night, not half that wholly dint'."

Meanwhile, also in Edition 5 of *The Merry Mawkin*, our newly-appointed technical adviser, **Stewart Orr**, wrote, under this heading:

On the recording trail for posterity

I was recently co-opted to the committee and I believe that my first job for FOND has been the best that anyone could wish – to go out and *spend* the cash from the grant that we so famously were awarded recently.

After much consultation and thought, both within the committee and with specialists without, FOND is now the owner of two complete minidisc recording systems. These comprise of a professional standard recorder, with a high quality radio reporter's microphone.

The recorders work either off rechargeable batteries, standard dry batteries or direct from the mains, and so can be used anywhere where the Norfolk dialect can be found.

Stewart Orr: FOND's technical adviser.

The whole set-up is of professional standard, so that any recordings we make will be good enough for any end user, provided the operators get things right. Each set is now housed in a smart varnished wooden flight case, custom-built for the recorders, and lined on the inside with plastic foam for protection.

There is an inventory of the contents of each case and anyone who uses them will be asked to attend a brief training session to ensure they don't damage anything. After all, each set cost us nearly £1,000 – and we want 'em to last!

In 2003, **Anne Doggett** was appointed as FOND's first sound archivist. Born and educated in Norwich, she trained as a librarian in Manchester, gaining a BA (Hons) in Library Studies in 1981.

She has held administrative and managerial posts in organisations in Norfolk and worked as a freelance indexer.

Anne was among 12 FOND members who in July, 2003, met at Stewart Orr's studios at Withersdale, near Harleston, for a technical briefing on the minidisc recording equipment.

Stewart wrote later: "The main business was to get to grips with the minidisc recording equipment owned by FOND. The session was aimed at teaching the rudiments of (a) operating equipment and (b) bringing back a good interview.

"Those present appeared to succeed in both aims (although the proof will be heard when the recordings they make start to trickle back to the studio)."

In addition to a cup of tea and a piece of cake, we were also honoured to receive a visit from Stewart's cat, bearer of surely the longest name in the feline world: Mstislav Harlequin Rostropovitch, Sir Felix the Inscrutable.

Shelagh Limmer's assistant, Mstislav Harlequin Rostropovitch, Sir Felix the Inscrutable, prepares to press the paws button.

CHAPTER 8

Two views of Norfolk

EIGHTEEN MONTHS before I introduced an occasional series to *The Merry Mawkin* called 'What Norfolk Means to Me', in which well-known Norfolk people expressed their thoughts on what made their home county special to them, I had contacted a former colleague of mine, **Ian Collins**, London correspondent of the *Eastern Daily Press*, one of its foremost journalists, authority on art and whose books include *A Broad Canvas: Art in East Anglia Since 1880* (Black Dog Books).

Ian Collins: 'Norfolk is a state of mind. I carry it with me.'

Norfolk-born Ian kindly provided an article which was to be the forerunner of the 'What Norfolk Means to Me' series, juxtaposing neatly with the already-established 'Norfolk by Adoption' feature. Here's what Ian wrote exclusively for *The Merry Mawkin* in 2001:

Our blessed county inspires a sense of camaraderie

While smugness is a sin, I've always felt fairly smirky because the Place of Birth slot on my passport is followed by the word Norwich.

" It's all very well for you to keep banging on about going back to your Norfolk roots," says my friend Alison. "I come from Birmingham and I couldn't wait to take the route marked Exit."

Oh yes, we're fortunate folk. Our blessed county inspires a sense of camaraderie, even in the most unlikely places... Even among former comrades. Once, on a train crossing from East Germany into Czechoslovakia in the depths of winter soon after the Warsaw Pact had imploded, I imagined myself in a scene from *Doctor Zhivago*. Or else on a one-way trip to Siberia in the era of Uncle Joe.

When the door of the ancient carriage was flung open by an armed guard, it was as if an Iron Curtain had parted. The intruder grabbed my passport, grunted and, pointing to the information beneath my photo, he bawled: "Not fill! Not fill!"

I thought he meant I hadn't filled in my signature, but as I searched vainly for a pen, Ivan the Unterrible began to smile. "Not *Phil* Collins!" he said. Ho hum. Ho, ho. The official was clearly an ardent Marxist (a fan of Groucho, Chico, Zeppo and Gummo, that is, rather than Karlo).

His manner had turned from fiendly to friendly in a flash, but when he noticed where I came from he broke into a broad grin and nearly broke my fingers in a handshake of welcome.

"Norwich City Football Club! Very good!" said my new best chum. Lucky he wasn't an Ipswich fan.

But I must confess that my locational loyalties are more widely drawn than the map of Norfolk. My flag is the three crowns of East Anglia. My mum's lot come from Suffolk and I was raised largely in Cambridgeshire.

Still, my paternal great-great-great grandfather was building boats in Coltishall around the time of Victoria's coronation.

And although the build-and-hire business was later floated to Wroxham, the family line continued down to my dad.

Those splendid wherry-yacht survivors, Olive and Norada, were built by my great-grandfather, but I wouldn't have a clue how to sail them, let alone repair them.

My father, however, retains a soft spot for the Olive. Repairing the leaky vessel back in the 1950s, he was standing knee-deep in freezing water and pondering the bleakness of being stony broke and unable to afford a key piece of fishing tackle.

Then, breaking through a plank of rotten timber, he found a flurry of lost silver and copper coins falling into his hand as if by magic. The mitt closed shut. And he reeled his way to the angling shop.

I love all that – and family memories of otter slides on the ice around Wroxham Broad and bitterns and swallowtail butterflies. And the sea. But now Norfolk is a state of mind. I carry it with me.

For seven of the ten years of FOND's existence, **Brenda Bizzell** has been our membership secretary, having been elected at the organisation's inaugural meeting at Yaxham Village Hall in October, 1999.

Brenda took a break between November, 2002, and November, 2005, when my wife Shelagh succeeded her during three of the four years of my editorship of *The Merry Mawkin*, enabling both offices to be conducted from the same address at Broome.

Brenda's 'Norfolk Wordsearch' puzzles have been a popular feature in the *Mawkin* ever since the autumn of 2001.

She contributed to the 'Norfolk by Adoption' series in Edition 5 in the winter of 2001:

NORFOLK BY ADOPTION: No 3 Brenda Bizzell

Some have Norfolk thrust upon them

Some are born in Norfolk, some move willingly to Norfolk, and some have Norfolk thrust upon them.

My parents moved here when I was 16 and, fresh out of school, I couldn't afford to stay a Londoner.

Having grown up believing London to be the centre of the universe and that foreigners started at Potters Bar, the culture shock was awful – and I spent the first three days crying. How

Brenda Bizzell serenading a Press Gang audience at Frettenham Village Hall. Bottom right of the picture: FOND's and the Press Gang's Colin Burleigh.

could I possibly survive in a village where you couldn't buy a newspaper and where there were only four buses a day?

The worst part of rural life was the nightly walk from the late bus – a long trudge through dark lanes, startled by every noise.

The night I slid along the road on squashed hedgehog remains was particularly unpleasant. I bought a torch after that.

My first job was with Norwich Union (wasn't everybody's in the 'sixties?) and due to my mantra of 'London wonderful – Norfolk awful', I was known as 'That B***** Londoner'. What a delightful companion I must have been.

When I achieved the freedom of Norfolk with a moped, my mood improved, although smelling of 'two-stroke oil' got me strange looks in the snootier areas of the office.

I found a new job at the River Authority and with it colleagues who were much more sympathetic to my strange ways and they persuaded me that Norfolk and its people were quite agreeable and could be fun.

Gradually I adjusted to the slower pace and enjoyed ambling through Norwich, finding that friends would have time to stop and talk. Shop assistants were prepared to be helpful and there was no elbowing and shoving on the pavements.

Times, sadly, have changed! Wednesdays were busier, being Market Day, which I couldn't understand, as Norwich Market

Place was open every day. When I learned the cattle market had just moved from the city centre, the thought of all those animals there scared me silly. I'd have stayed home every Wednesday.

I didn't know I loved Norfolk until I left it. My fate was sealed at St Benet's Abbey, where I joined a work camp to shore up church and riverbanks, and met my future husband.

He lived in Exeter, so off I went, only to be homesick – but for Norfolk, not London. More sobbing, and we agreed to move 'home'. I made the excuse that we'd be much closer to the oil industry, and travelling would be easier.

In truth, I'd grown roots and didn't like pulling them up. We've been back for 23 years now, so hopefully I may soon be excused my temporary absence and granted citizenship.

My London accent hasn't disappeared, though it's half way up the A140 now and I'm told I 'go Norfolk' when talking to friends. 'That B***** Londoner' is now someone who knows when she's on to a good thing.

Please, Mr Skipper, can I have my Norfolk passport now?

CHAPTER 9

UEA honours FOND president

IN THE SPRING of 2002 *The Merry Mawkin* proudly announced that FOND president **Professor Peter Trudgill** would be receiving an Honorary Doctorate from the University of East Anglia on July 11.

Professor Trudgill said he liked to think that the LittD (Doctor of Letters) was 'a bit of recognition for FOND as well'.

"It is due recognition," wrote Tony Clarke in the *Mawkin*, "in his own county, for an acknowledged international expert on English linguistics who reveals with pride that 'all of my great-great-grandparents came from eastern Norfolk'."

Born at Thorpe St Andrew in 1943 and educated at the City of Norwich School, Peter was awarded his BA at King's College, Cambridge, in 1966 and a PhD at Edinburgh University in 1971.

Professor Peter Trudgill, president of Friends of Norfolk Dialect.

His university teaching career has taken him to Reading (1970–86), Essex (1986–92) and Lausanne, Switzerland (1992–98). At the time of writing in 2002, he was Professor of English Linguistics at the University of Fribourg, Switzerland, where he remained until retirement in 2005.

Professor Trudgill is a Fellow of the British Academy, and the thirty or more books he has either written or edited include

The Norfolk Dialect in Poppyland Publishing's 'Norfolk Origins' series; *The Social Differentiation of English in Norwich* (published in 1974); *The Dialects of England* (Amazon); *Sociolinguistics: An Introduction to Language and Society* (Penguin Books) and *Sociolinguistic Variation and Change* (Edinburgh University Press).

Tony Clarke, in the *Mawkin* article, added: "All FOND friends, basking in a kind of reflected glory, will undoubtedly be pleased to congratulate our president on his honorary doctorate.

"Even though he has gone to furrin parts in the past few years (Fribourg is even further from home than Ipswich!) he has proved that a prophet is not without honour in his own county."

An example of the regular academic articles on dialect which Professor Trudgill contributed to *The Merry Mawkin* is this one which appeared in the same edition as the one that announced his Honorary Doctorate from the UEA, spring, 2002:

PROFESSOR PETER TRUDGILL DISCUSSES THE VARIED USAGE OF THE CONJUNCTION *DO*

Do: 3-stage two-letter word in our dialect has link with a US state

In the older dialects of East Anglia, the word *do* is used as a conjunction which means something like *otherwise*.

The *English Dialect Dictionary* shows that this usage was once found in the dialects of Norfolk, Suffolk, Cambridgeshire and northern Essex.

How did this form develop? The answer seems to be that it is an example of what linguists call *grammaticalisation*, in which words increasingly come to be used in a more abstract and grammatical way

Consider the following:

Don't you take yours off, do you'll get rheumatism.

Don't you tell your Aunt Agatha about the coupons, do she'll mob me.

In these examples, the insertion of *because if you* will provide forms readily comprehensible to speakers of all English dialects:

Don't take yours off, [because if you] ***do you'll get rheumatism.***

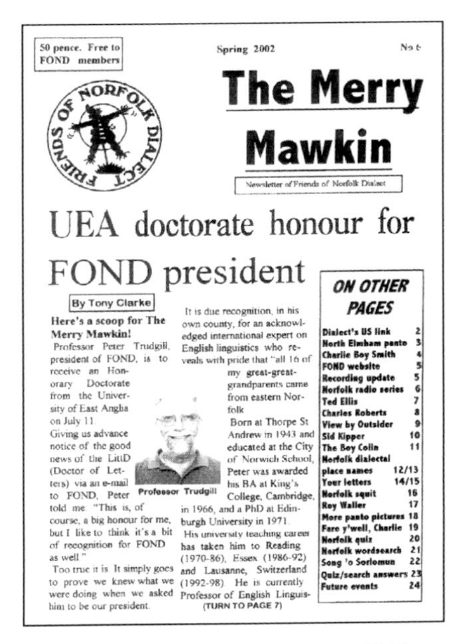

50 pence. Free to FOND members

Spring 2002 No 6

The Merry Mawkin

Newsletter of Friends of Norfolk Dialect

UEA doctorate honour for FOND president

By Tony Clarke

Here's a scoop for The Merry Mawkin!

Professor Peter Trudgill, president of FOND, is to receive an Honorary Doctorate from the University of East Anglia on July 11.

Giving us advance notice of the good news of the LittD (Doctor of Letters) via an e-mail to FOND, Peter told me: "This is, of course, a big honour for me, but I like to think it's a bit of recognition for FOND as well."

Too true it is. It simply goes to prove we knew what we were doing when we asked him to be our president.

Professor Trudgill

It is due recognition, in his own county, for an acknowledged international expert on English linguistics who reveals with pride that "all 16 of my great-great-grandparents came from eastern Norfolk.

Born at Thorpe St Andrew in 1943 and educated at the City of Norwich School, Peter was awarded his BA at King's College, Cambridge, in 1966, and a PhD at Edinburgh University in 1971.

His university teaching career has taken him to Reading (1970-86), Essex (1986-92) and Lausanne, Switzerland (1992-98). He is currently Professor of English Linguis-

(TURN TO PAGE 7)

ON OTHER PAGES

The Merry Mawkin: spring issue 2002.

It seems, then, that the development of the conjunction *do* began with an initial stage in which speakers simply omitted phrases such as *because if.*

This is not the end of the story, however. A second stage in the development of a more abstract meaning can be illustrated by the following:

Have the fox left? No that ain't, do Bailey would've let them went.

Here the link between the two parts of the sentence is more abstract and complicated. The originally present-tense form *do* is being applied in a past-tense context, and *do* is used in spite of the fact that we would have to insert a form of *have*, not *do*, to get a full form of the sentence:

No that ain't [because if that had] ***Bailey would've let them went.***

The third and final stage in the process is demonstrated in examples like:

That's a good job we come out of that there field, do he'd've had us!

We stabled them elephants right in the middle, do we should've capsized.

Here present-tense *do* is once again being used in past-tense contexts, but it is also being used in spite of the fact it is a positive verb form, in a situation where a full form of the sentence would require a negative verb:

That's a good job we came out of that there field, [because if we hadn't] ***he'd've had us!***

The conjunction *do* is not found anywhere in the British Isles outside East Anglia. Nor, as far as I know, is it found anywhere else in the English-speaking world, with one exception – the south-eastern United States.

One of the *Dictionary of American Regional English (DARE)* informants writes: 'In eastern North Carolina, during the period approximately from 1915–1930, I remember hearing white people, speakers with moderate education, saying things like:

Shut the door tight, do *it'll blow open before morning* and *leave the note in the middle of the table,* do *she won't see it.*

It would be reasonable to assume that the conjunction *do* arrived in North Carolina in the speech of immigrants from East Anglia.

Interested readers can learn more about this and other dialect features in Peter Trudgill's Edinburgh University Press book *Sociolinguistic Variation and Change*.

CHAPTER 10

www.norfolkdialect.com

YES, WE'VE MADE IT – our own website: www.norfolkdialect.com! In the spring of 2002, FOND's technical adviser, **Stewart Orr**, announced in Edition 6 of *The Merry Mawkin*:

> Towards the end of last year the committee agreed to authorise the design of a website to publicise the activities and aims of FOND.
>
> Two members were encouraged to put forward design proposals and soon produced a draft site. The site is now fully functional and contains:
>
> *An introduction by our chairman, who has also made mention of the site on local radio and in the *Eastern Daily Press*.
>
> *A summary of the aims of FOND.
>
> *A summary of the current edition of *The Merry Mawkin*, which will be updated as appropriate.
>
> *A membership form enabling potential members to download it and join.
>
> *A number of links to various related and relevant sites.
>
> It is intended to include sound files, photographs, etc, and a Norfolk dictionary has been suggested for inclusion. Further suggestions are welcomed.
>
> We hope you will all visit the site, encourage your friends to visit it and sign the guestbook.

Pauline Dodd; FOND's first website co-ordinator.

Within a month, some 700 'hits' had already been received.

The FOND website was off to a good start and under the guidance of its indomitable co-ordinator, **Pauline Dodd**, has proved an unqualified success. Indeed, by the spring of 2009 the number of hits registered had reached more than 77,000.

Very quickly, we found that Norfolk exiles from all over the world were getting in touch with us and some interesting correspondence was published each quarter in the *Mawkin*, but one particularly fascinating story originated not that far away from Norfolk – in Oxford.

In 2002 Daniel Bennett was a trainee solicitor in this university city but it seemed his real ambition was to be an actor. He had landed a part in an Oxford Theatre Guild production of a play called *The Sea*, but, as he saw it, he had a problem.

The Sea, by Edward Bond, is a tragi-comedy set on the East Coast shortly before the First World War and Daniel's role was Hollarcut, a country character caught up in traumatic events. Daniel's problem was that when he tried to sound like an East Anglian his accents came out West Country. The dreaded Mummerzet, bane of all our lives, was rearing its ugly head.

So Daniel surfed the net – and promptly made history as the first actor to be helped through FOND's new website.

His plea for help was taken up by FOND secretary Tony Clarke and myself as *Merry Mawkin* editor. Daniel sent blank tapes and with equipment I normally use for recording items for the *Three Rivers Talking Newspaper for the Blind* in the Bungay, Beccles, Halesworth and Loddon area, we produced a cassette in which Tony's 'Boy Jimma' enunciated Daniel's script in the purest of broad Norfolk.

This was duly sent off to Daniel and then, while cycling to work through Oxford's busy streets each morning, he had the Boy Jimma's dulcet tones ringing in his ears via his personal headphones.

Somehow, he survived unscathed and the play enjoyed a successful five-night run at the Oxford Playhouse. And by a happy coincidence, Tony, his wife Pat and their younger son Tim happened to be in Oxford for a family celebration and were in the audience for the last-night performance.

The Boy Jimma commented afterwards: "Daniel din't mearke much of a fist of a Norfolk accent, but at least he hed a proper go. More o' them actors shud dew wot he dun an' try an' git FOND ter help 'em git that right."

Just after FOND had come to the aid of one budding actor, we found ourselves engaged in a similar operation with another – this time, however, instead of someone less than 200 miles from Norfolk it was a young lady living on the other side of the world, more than 12,000 miles away, in New Zealand!

This story began when Mrs Mildred Moss, of Southtown, Great Yarmouth, wrote to FOND chairman Keith Skipper in the autumn of 2002:

> "This morning I got in touch with Radio Norfolk and they very kindly gave me your address.
>
> "I have a friend in New Zealand who has gone blind and her daughter, Jocelyn Mangin, is in a play and it requires Norfolk dialect.
>
> "I will appreciate your kindness if you would translate on the enclosed tape the Norfolk dialect. She has underlined the parts she plays.
>
> "Thank you for your kind attention.
>
> "Mildred Moss."

Keith then 'phoned me and I contacted a friend at Halesworth, Rene Pearce, a retired teacher who was born at Dereham and coincidentally was a childhood neighbour of Colin Burleigh, of FOND and Press Gang fame, The Boy Colin. Rene, well-versed in the Norfolk dialect, was just the person to record the dialogue for Jocelyn from Te Aroha, North Island, New Zealand.

After recording Rene's readings and adding an extract from Tony Clarke's tape of his Boy Jimma book, *Mighta Bin Wuss*, I sent the tape to Mrs Moss at Yarmouth, who forwarded it to Jocelyn across the globe.

Soon I received the following e-mail from New Zealand:

> "Just a short note to say thanks for the tape which I received through Mildred Moss. It is wonderful to see how small things reach such a long way. My name is Jocelyn Mangin and I have a small part in this play which is being put on by the little theatre in the little town where I live.
>
> "The town is called Te Aroha, which is in the middle of farming country in the North Island of New Zealand.
>
> "I was tickled to get this part as I was, in fact, born at Great Yarmouth, spent my childhood in Zambia and then emigrated to New Zealand with my family.
>
> "So I have a link with you all in that part of the world. Thank you so much again for your help. I know that hearing your tape will help me more than you can imagine.
>
> "Regards,
>
> "Jocelyn."

I asked Jocelyn for a follow-up and a few weeks later I received this e-mail:

> "Just a short note to let you know that the play, *Vinegar Tom*, has finished its run and was a great success. I was very grateful for the tape which was so very helpful. I simply played it over and over and learned parrot-style.
>
> "I have found the whole exercise a great learning curve, quite a challenge for me, and there was some comment from the audience as to how authentic my accent sounded.
>
> "I have passed the tape on to the local speech teacher. She thought it would be a great teaching aid. I am thrilled that we have been able to make contact over this.
>
> "Isn't it wonderful that we are a million miles away but all part of the one world!
>
> "Thank you again,
>
> "Jocelyn Mangin."

And just to complete a trilogy of similar stories, in the same edition of the *Mawkin*, in the winter of 2002, we reported:

> The National Arts Centre in Ottawa has also benefited from a selection of authentic Norfolk voices.
>
> Eileen Leiper, of North Walsham, contacted Keith Skipper on behalf of her daughter Moira in Canada. She was anxious to encourage the 'right sort' of Norfolk sound for a forthcoming Ottawa production which called for accents heard in this county.
>
> Keith provided copies of the *Norfolk Echoes* CD he compiled in partnership with Stewart Orr – and the recordings were sent out immediately, in the name of true culture.

Tony Clarke's Boy Jimma book, Mighta Bin Wuss, published in 1998.

In his foreword, Keith Skipper wrote: 'This is no roses-round-the-door pastoral eulogy penned by a rustic remnant leaning on the broken gatepost of times past. It is a stirring tribute to a fast vanishing world which fashioned virtues out of austerity and found humour in adversity. Truly squit, wit – and plenty more.'

CHAPTER 11

New chairman

UNDER THE SOCIETY'S CONSTITUTION, FOND's chairmen must retire after three years, and so at the AGM in Yaxham Village Hall on October 27, 2002 it was time for our first chairman, Keith Skipper, to stand down and make way for **Peter Brooks**, who had succeeded Martin Kirby as vice-chairman in 2000.

Reflecting on three eventful and successful years since the organisation's formation, Keith wrote:

> After that momentous meeting on Sunday, October 3, 1999, packed with local pride and optimism, I noted in my diary: 'A day for celebration, a day I hope future generations will salute with gratitude'.
>
> Perhaps I got carried away by all the excitement, but the use of such heady language seems to have been vindicated by subsequent events.
>
> This is a flourishing organisation making a mark well beyond Norfolk's boundaries. We have our own website, underlining the value of combining modern technology with traditional virtues, and a newsletter that has blossomed into a powerful and entertaining voice for the cause.
>
> A lottery windfall of nearly £4,000 has paved the way for a precious recording programme, key components in the crusade to preserve our dialect for future generations. We are forging close links with county archivist Dr John Alban and the Norfolk Record Office.
>
> Our president, Professor Peter Trudgill, has been honoured by the University of East Anglia. We will continue to explore the

academic side of linguistics while maintaining our passion for the humour and homeliness of our native tongue.

To this end, the FOND-dew wagon must continue to roll round the county, mixing the serious with a bit of squit in a sociable setting.

Peter Brooks; elected FOND chairman in October, 2002, succeeding Keith Skipper.

Perhaps support will grow for an annual dinner or some other formal celebration in years to come. Of course there are areas for improvement. It is hard to get the dialect message into local schools – and we desperately need teachers and youngsters to pick up these heritage threads – while the old Mummerzet murmurings can still be heard on national radio and television.

Too many people pay FOND lip service without taking the trouble to join. That sort of patronising could prove fatal. Even so, there's so much cause for pride over what has been achieved in three busy years.

The enthusiasm, energy and expertise of officers, committee members and supporters have laid perfect foundations for a healthy future.

It has been a privilege and a pleasure to play a part in the beginnings of a great Norfolk adventure.

Our new chairman, Peter Brooks, wrote in the *Mawkin's* winter edition, 2002:

It does not seem three years since a small band of enthusiasts called a public meeting at Yaxham Village Hall to consider what could be done to stem the tide of 'Mummerzet' which was increasingly flowing through radio and TV programmes in which producers mistakenly thought they were portraying a Norfolk accent.

Keith Skipper was elected as our first chairman and he deserves the thanks of all who love the Norfolk dialect for the way in which he has steered our new society through the turbulent waters always present when a new group is launched.

Thank you, Keith, you will be a hard act to follow.

We are now well and truly established, are recognised at county level as having something positive to contribute to Norfolk's cultural diversity, have a solid membership base and have successfully proclaimed the importance of an understanding and appreciation for preserving our native tongue in a materialistic world.

We must build on the sound foundations laid. Our president is compiling *The Norfolk Dialect*, a book which, from what I've seen of a first draft, should be a best seller.

We will continue our discussions with educationists regarding the possibility of introducing Norfolk dialect into local school curricula, co-operate with radio and TV producers to replace Mummerzet with authentic Norfolk dialect, expand our programme of social 'dews' across the county and continue to work with the Norfolk Cultural Strategy team to gain wider support for our declared aims of encouraging the preservation and protection of the Norfolk dialect and to study its history and usage. We will do all we can to promote and advance its use.

We need to expand our programme of interviewing people to record examples of genuine Norfolk dialect, to establish if there might be support for a Norfolk dialect residential weekend school, possibly an annual dinner and perhaps develop links with dialect societies nationwide.

We have our very own 'groupies' who follow us from venue to venue, but we do need more members. So, persuade a friend, twist a relative's arm and work your wiles on unsuspecting neighbours – they will soon come to thank you for parting with the modest membership fee! Honest! The stronger we become the more influence we will have.

Peter Brooks was well suited to become chairman of FOND. He was born at Dereham, and like his predecessor, Keith Skipper, attended Hamond's Grammar School, Swaffham.

While studying in London to qualify as an environmental health officer, he worked in the housing department of Epsom and Ewell Borough Council.

On qualifying, Peter moved to Warwickshire in 1951 and was with Southam Rural District Council till 1955 when he returned to Norfolk to Docking RDC and from 1958–63 he was with Smallburgh RDC at Stalham.

He then moved to Sheringham-based Erpingham RDC where from 1963–74 he was chief environmental health officer, serving also with the RDC's successor, North Norfolk District Council.

From 1974–81 he was public relations officer with East Staffordshire District Council and from 1981–93 worked with publishing companies.

Since 1988 Peter has been vice-chairman and curator of Sheringham Museum. A past chairman of Museums in Norfolk Group(MING), he represents independent museums in Norfolk on Norfolk County Council's Joint Museums Committee and is a co-opted member of North Norfolk Area Museums Committee.

He is author of eight local history books, an A-level textbook on international environment topics and a history of London's Pearly Kings and Queens. He has contributed to the *Eastern Daily Press Saturday Magazine*, *Let's Talk!* magazine, the *Norfolk Journal* and other regional and national publications.

Peter is married, has three daughters, one son and six grandchildren.

CHAPTER 12

The Baroness

AMONG THOSE ATTENDING the AGM in Yaxham Village Hall on October 27, 2002, when the new chairman was elected, was the MP for South-West Norfolk and former Cabinet Minister, **Gillian Shephard**.

This was, of course, before her elevation to the peerage when she became Baroness Shephard of Northwold. The then Mrs Shephard was there to deliver a very entertaining talk – despite the fact that she had recently suffered a broken leg and had had to brave the worst gale since 1987 to get there!

It was also the day that Mrs Shephard and her husband Tom became members of FOND.

After the meeting, I asked her if she would write an article to appear in a future edition of *The Merry Mawkin*. Without hesitation, she said she would be delighted to do so.

Incidentally, regarding the gale on the day of our annual meeting, **Tony Clarke** wrote in the lead story of *The Merry Mawkin's* bumper 28-page winter edition, just before Christmas, 2002:

> Most voluntary organisations would be glad to get 40 or so members to their annual meeting. Imagine getting that number on a day when Norfolk was suffering its worst gale since 1987 and many of those members had to travel from various far-flung corners of the county and beyond.
>
> Given that sort of imagination, you might have heard, carried on the wind, the distant cry: 'Blast thass a-blowin' fit ter blind yer!' as trees fell everywhere, blocking roads and bringing down power lines.

Baroness Shephard, a member of FOND.

The thousands whose homes were plunged back into the dark ages of Tilley lamps and candles included former Cabinet Minister, long-serving MP and general 'good ow' Norfolk mawther', Gillian Shephard.

As if that wasn't bad enough, Mrs Shephard also had a broken leg. But, in the true do-or-die spirit of Norfolk people, FOND's meeting went ahead, and Mrs Shephard, grateful for the warmth and light of Yaxham Village Hall, delivered a highly entertaining talk.

And afterwards she and her husband became members of FOND.

Following her promise at the AGM, I wrote to Mrs Shephard, asking if she could kindly contribute a piece for the spring edition. Only five days later, I received, from her office at the House of Commons, a letter in which she wrote:

> "I am delighted to do this, and enclose the article herewith!
> "With every good wish.
> "Yours ever,
> "Gillian Shephard."

If you want something done, ask a busy person...

And this is the article which Mrs Shephard, soon to be Baroness, wrote exclusively for Edition 9 of *The Merry Mawkin* in the spring of 2003:

Thank goodness for FOND, says Gillian Shephard

Every time I visit a school, or talk to young people locally, I am struck by their lack of a Norfolk accent. In some ways their speech is more correct than a broad Norfolk accent, but with the cockney overtones, the interrogative ends to sentences which are not questions, and the frequent glottal stop, their speech is more like their peers' in other parts of Britain than like that of their parents, or grandparents.

When I was at school, we were taught to be bilingual. As someone who went on to be a linguist, I was perhaps more interested than most in our ability to switch from one mode to another, and in the contrast there already was between our language and that of our older relatives.

Baroness Shephard and her husband Tom.

Our family used some extraordinary words, some of which I suspect were 'Romany' rather than Norfolk words. Parney was used for rain, dannocks for gloves and cushies for sweets.

My grandmother always referred to highmagulls (those of high birth or in charge), and to desabills (what you wore before you got dressed).

Tricolate was in common usage, from tricolour, or so my

Oxford French tutor told me. Dodman was always used for snail, and dickey for donkey. Maufrodite was used for a kind of wagon which could be used for various purposes, and obviously, also for a hermaphrodite animal. One of my favourite words was blunk, used for a heavy fall of snow, although that may have been purely a family word.

On the other hand, it is clearly onomatopoeic. Does anyone use it, I wonder? Vocabulary is one thing, usage, sentence form, expression are others.

Norfolk people, anyway from the north-east of the county, are not known for their garrulity. Brevity, especially in the put-down, is the essence of Norfolk speech.

Thus the late Dick Bagnall-Oakeley, of blessèd memory, records meeting someone on a freezing February day on a north Norfolk beach.

As they struggled past each other, the stranger said to Dick, "Sweatin'?"

Sidney Grapes, of equally blessèd renown, insisted that we are so brief because of the wind. Will we change with global warming?

What is clear is that with what is nothing short of an agricultural and economic revolution in our own county going on, much of our cultural richness and diversity risks extinction.

Think of all the language devoted to the care of horses, the blacksmith, and the unmechanised harvest that is already lost. How much can we remember between us?

Thank goodness for FOND. Let's collect all we can remember, together!

CHAPTER 13

The Lord Lieutenant

HAVING ESTABLISHED THE SERIES 'Norfolk by Adoption' – eight episodes by the summer *Mawkin* of 2003 – I decided to run, in parallel, a new regular feature, 'What Norfolk Means to Me', in which well-known Norfolk people would express their thoughts on what makes their home county special to them.

For the first contribution, I went to the top. I asked **Sir Timothy Colman**, Lord Lieutenant of Norfolk – the Queen's representative in the county. He was also chairman of Eastern Counties Newspapers Group (now Archant), my employer when I worked on the *Eastern Daily Press*. He is, moreover, a vice-president of FOND.

Sir Timothy kindly agreed to write the first article in the new series, 'What Norfolk Means to Me', for Edition 10 of *The Merry Mawkin* in the summer of 2003.

Once again, I had found that if you want something done, ask a busy person... (with one exception – see Chapter 37).

And here are Sir Timothy's thoughts on his home county:

Why the loyalty of Norfolk citizens is exceptional

I have been asked by the editor of *The Merry Mawkin* to write a few words about 'what Norfolk means to me'. Like many others, I suspect, I know the answer but it's neither in my nature nor easy to explain it on paper!

Norfolk is very special. The support for FOND has been astonishing and continues to grow. That itself tells a story. Support from many who were born in Norfolk, as I was, but equally significant from hundreds of others who have moved to the county, absorbed its characteristic charms and now share a determination that the best elements of its individuality should be cherished and sheltered from the creeping conformity which plagues our world.

Sir Timothy Colman, a vice-president of FOND.

There can be little doubt that the place of your birth and childhood has a strong influence, and will always mean a lot to any individual.

A man born in Devon, for example, I would expect to have a deep loyalty to that county. What is remarkable about Norfolk, however, is that the loyalty of its citizens is, I believe, exceptional when compared to others. Why is this?

Our surroundings, I've no doubt, are part of the story – the wide open skies, the special light, the physical independence from the rest of the country. Who was it who said many years ago that Norfolk was protected from the north and east by the sea, and the south and west by the LNER (the old London and North-Eastern Railway)?

People don't pass through Norfolk, they come for a purpose. The line stops at Cromer. I accept that it doesn't help our economic prospects, but it does much to preserve the county's culture.

Direct exposure to the sea, wonderful beaches, migrating birds easily viewed, the gentle hills which are a surprise to many, and of course the history and romance of the Broads, so well epitomised by Arthur Ransome.

What other corner of England prompted a group of artists, mostly local born, and landscapists to draw common inspiration from their surrounds and form the famous Norwich School? They captured the wherries, groves of trees, meadows, beach scenes and bridges of the early 19th century.

Above all, that unique feature of the Norfolk landscape – its 650 medieval churches with the Norman Cathedral at the centre now approaching 1,000 years old. Drive 30 miles in any direction and they will present themselves to you one after another.

Step inside and breathe the history of this region. Visit the bustling market towns, each with its own charm.

But without any doubt it is the ordinary people of Norfolk throughout its history who have been its backbone and have certainly meant most to me since I was a small boy.

Boadicea, Horatio Nelson, Coxswain Henry Blogg, one has read about, but Jim Vincent at Hickling, who introduced me to the bittern; Ted Ellis, who was an encyclopaedia of natural history knowledge as well as an enchanting communicator, and Joe Abel, who looked after my grandfather's pony and trap and drove us as children all round the farm on which I was brought up.

Helping to stook the oats and loading the tumbril pulled by a Suffolk Punch before building a stack which would stand for the winter. These were some of the true Norfolk experiences I shall never forget.

Which brings me back to the Norfolk character, that independence of spirit, very special humour and economy of words. I guess Norfolk has suffered more and varied invasions than most other parts of the country, so we are not thoroughbreds!

The county is a mosaic of foreign influences which may account for its strongly individual character.

Remember that as recently as the 17th century Norwich was the second largest city in England. The coastline, Broads, Breckland, churches – flint cottages, huge skies. They all spell Norfolk to me. But so does the dynamism of its contemporary culture, with university, museums, music, theatre, Forum, industry and leisure.

Good luck and more power to the elbow of Friends of Norfolk Dialect.

CHAPTER 14

The Deputy Lieutenant

HAVING FEATURED the Lord Lieutenant of Norfolk in the 2003 summer edition of *The Merry Mawkin*, by coincidence the next publication was to spotlight a newly-appointed Deputy Lieutenant of the county – our very own **Keith Skipper**!

It was the *Eastern Daily Press* which broke the news on July 25 with the headline:

Squit and polish in Mr Norfolk's society role – Keith Skipper tells of pleasure at joining ranks of deputy lieutenants

Reporter Shaun Lowthorpe, introducing the story, wrote:

Keith Skipper, labourer's son and Norfolk wit, often pillories the great and the good of the county. But yesterday he joined the higher echelons of county society when he was appointed a deputy lieutenant."

The *EDP* report continued:

Every year the Lord Lieutenant of Norfolk – the Queen's representative in the county – seeks out people to stand in for him when he is away or advise him on a range of matters.

Generally, the appointments are publicised, then quickly forgotten. The deputy lieutenants have no specific public duties.

They no longer wear official robes and the post is unpaid.

But the five deputies appointed by Sir Timothy Colman on Wednesday certainly have the common touch.

Sir Timothy said yesterday that the deputies had always been chosen from a diverse field and were a vital source of advice and information.

"The object is to help maintain the Lord Lieutenancy effectively and be as widely representative of the county's life," he said. "Deputy lieutenants are widely representative of the county in many respects, including location, gender, social range and service – particularly voluntary service within the community."

The latest batch – Norfolk-man Keith Skipper, former Education Secretary Gillian Shephard, magistrate and *EDP* 'We Care' chairwoman Paddy Seligman, ex-Lord Mayor of Norwich Brenda Ferris and King's Lynn Preservation Trust chairman Anthony Williams – seems more high-profile than usual.

But maybe it should come as no surprise – after all we give gongs to Sir Elton John, Sir Alex Ferguson and Dame Judi Dench, so maybe there is a trickle-down effect which is seeping towards the shires.

Keith Skipper, who was born and brought up in a tied cottage at Beeston, near Dereham, as one of a family of ten, said he was honoured to have been appointed a deputy.

He will be among the forty people who currently hold the post of deputy, including Baroness Hollis, Lady Knollys and Barry Capon, the former chief executive of Norfolk County Council.

Mr Skipper said: "At last, a little bit of polish to go with all the squit.

"Seriously, it is extremely gratifying to find appreciation in significant quarters for my unashamed passion for Norfolk – a passion that has cost me dear on some occasions."

And he said that, despite the accolade, he had no plans to change or adopt any airs and graces!

"I have always regarded pure parochialism as a quality to be applauded rather than a weakness to be criticised. I don't think there are many areas in between.

Conference Centre on 14 July and this was my report, as lead story in Edition 11 of *The Merry Mawkin*, autumn, 2003:

Dialect course success 'stimulating, very much a starting point'

By Robin Limmer

The FOND dream came true! Teachers from many parts of Norfolk, together with other educationists, academics and members of FOND gathered at Easton College in July to hear from two internationally-renowned linguistics experts on the validity of all regional accents and dialects in English and the impact of the Norfolk dialect on the county's children.

A similar seminar the next day at King's Lynn was also well supported at West Norfolk Professional Development Centre. Both were organised by the Norfolk Education Advisory Service.

The star attractions at this unprecedented occasion were FOND's president, Professor Peter Trudgill, Chair of English Linguistics at the University of Fribourg, Switzerland, and Dr Ken Lodge, Senior Lecturer in Linguistics and Phonetics at the University of East Anglia.

"Words don't often fail me, and they won't fail me now," said Chris Snudden, head of literacy, Norfolk Education Department, after the first day, "but I do have to say that this has been one of the most interesting days that I've spent for a long, long time.

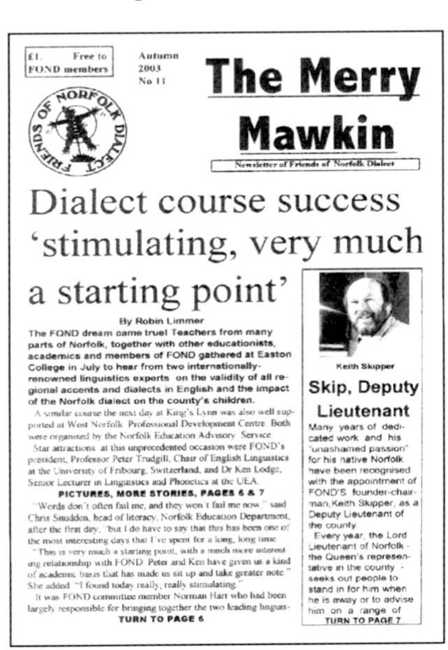

£1. Free to FOND members

Autumn 2003 No 11

The Merry Mawkin

Newsletter of Friends of Norfolk Dialect

Dialect course success 'stimulating, very much a starting point'

By Robin Limmer

The FOND dream came true! Teachers from many parts of Norfolk, together with other educationists, academics and members of FOND gathered at Easton College in July to hear from two internationally-renowned linguistics experts on the validity of all regional accents and dialects in English and the impact of the Norfolk dialect on the county's children.

A similar course the next day at King's Lynn was also well supported at West Norfolk Professional Development Centre. Both were organised by the Norfolk Education Advisory Service.

Star attractions at this unprecedented occasion were FOND's president, Professor Peter Trudgill, Chair of English Linguistics at the University of Fribourg, Switzerland, and Dr Ken Lodge, Senior Lecturer in Linguistics and Phonetics at the UEA.

PICTURES, MORE STORIES, PAGES 6 & 7

"Words don't often fail me, and they won't fail me now," said Chris Snudden, head of literacy, Norfolk Education Department, after the first day, "but I do have to say that this has been one of the most interesting days that I've spent for a long, long time.

"This is very much a starting point, with a much more interesting relationship with FOND. Peter and Ken have given us a kind of academic basis that has made us sit up and take greater note." She added "I found today really, really stimulating."

It was FOND committee member Norman Hart who had been largely responsible for bringing together the two leading linguis-

TURN TO PAGE 6

Keith Skipper

Skip, Deputy Lieutenant

Many years of dedicated work and his "unashamed passion" for his native Norfolk have been recognised with the appointment of FOND'S founder-chairman, Keith Skipper, as a Deputy Lieutenant of the county.

Every year, the Lord Lieutenant of Norfolk - the Queen's representative in the county - seeks out people to stand in for him when he is away or to advise him on a range of

TURN TO PAGE 7

The Merry Mawkin: autumn issue 2003.

"This is very much a starting point, with a much more interesting relationship with FOND. Peter and Ken have given us a kind of academic basis that has made us sit up and take greater note." She added: "I found today really, really stimulating."

It was FOND committee member Norman Hart who had been largely responsible for bringing together the two leading linguistics and academics with head teachers, heads of English and English co-ordinators.

Professor Trudgill praised retired teacher Norman's pioneering work. "Norman," he said, "was particularly instrumental in saying, 'Why don't we actually do something to combine the people who are really doing the work of teaching English language with FOND and the academic and linguistic community?'

"Thanks especially to Norman and to the other members of FOND."

Chris Snudden also said that one of her jobs as head of literacy was to set up training for teachers in English, both primary and secondary.

"There is an increasing culture in the way in which we work where it's felt we don't really need to know why, we just need to teach children to do this. And it's leading to an awful lot of sometimes very mechanistic approaches.

"I'm a Norfolk girl myself and I feel we are losing some of the richness, some of the culture and some of the value we should be placing on many things, not just language.

"What I can guarantee is that I'll continue to take this day forward in as many ways as possible to set up opportunities, and if any of you individually want to set up opportunities yourselves, I know Norman will be very keen to talk to you, because there are people in FOND who would be willing to work with teachers and I'm sure even pupils in this area, but I personally will be taking this forward as well."

FOND chairman Peter Brooks thanked Professor Trudgill and Dr Lodge, and the organisers, Chris Snudden and Anna McCarthy, Arts in Education Project Development Officer.

"It's been a highlight in our development of FOND and we

look forward to working with Chris and Anna to see what contributions we can make," he said.

In his address to the conference, Dr Ken Lodge, Senior Lecturer in Linguistics and Phonetics at the UEA, asked:

Where do accents come from?

"Where do all these accents and dialects come from? They don't come from anywhere. They've always been there, from the year dot.

"You've got two kinds of change. There's the internal mechanism change which can be explained in terms of children not attaining the exact target.

"The parents to start with are the target of their acquisition of language. That doesn't last very long, because by the time they're four or five they're socialising, they're more interested in sounding like their pals than their parents.

"The other change is the external change. Certain things happen from the outside and this may cause terrific language change."

Dr Lodge said the Norman invasion in 1066 resulted in French being imposed on top of English, so a lot of aspects of English were heavily influenced by French.

Professor Peter Trudgill spoke of the influence of London on Norfolk and other dialects:

London origin of our Ws and Vs

"Everybody in the Norfolk education system, whether teachers or pupils, speaks some kind of dialect.

"When we're talking about the Norfolk dialect from the point of view of the education system, we're not just talking about the traditional Norfolk dialect that we associate with the Boy John Letters or books about traditional Norfolk dialect.

"Recently there had been reference to the influence of London on Norfolk and other dialects."

This was not new, said the professor. The old Norfolk

pronunciation of W for V (*willage* or *wittals*) originated in London. For instance, Dickens' Sam Weller used this form. It died out in London around 1900 but continued in Norfolk. "So something we think of as a Norfolk dialect feature actually came from London."

Whither Standard English?

"Why teach non-Standard-English-speaking children to write and read Standard English?" asked Professor Trudgill. "No good reason except the social reason.

"There is a very strong social convention in this country where everybody who is supposed to be educated is supposed to be able to use Standard English and it's really almost a definitional matter...

"I think we should feel a bit uncomfortable about teaching people to write Standard English. Obviously we should do it, but whether we should teach people to *speak* Standard English is another matter."

So concluded a very successful and productive, first-ever Norfolk dialect seminar, a meeting of minds of linguistics experts, teachers, county educationists and, indeed, members of Friends of Norfolk Dialect.

It was to lead, quite quickly and dramatically, to a major development – the introduction into Norfolk schools of a programme enabling teachers and pupils to appreciate the importance of dialect and how Standard English has grown out of it.

And it's not surprising that Norman Hart, who had played such a pioneering part in this achievement, was appointed FOND's education officer.

CHAPTER 17

Seminars' sequel

So, as the sequel to the highly successful dialect seminars at Easton College and King's Lynn, *The Merry Mawkin* was able to announce proudly on its 2003 winter edition front page:

Dialect programme for Norfolk schools

By Tony Clarke

The Norfolk Education Advisory Service is to introduce a programme into schools to enable teachers and pupils to appreciate the importance of dialect and how Standard English has grown out of it.

Reporting this at FOND's annual meeting on October 26 at Yaxham Village Hall, chairman Peter Brooks said the move followed the two successful seminars for teachers and other educationists conducted by our president, Professor Peter Trudgill, and Dr Ken Lodge, Senior Lecturer in Linguistics and Phonetics at the University of East Anglia.

Praising the work of FOND education officer Norman Hart, Peter Brooks said: "Norman and I have, this past week, had a meeting with the head of literacy, Norfolk Education Department, to discuss how FOND may be able to help in building up this programme."

He spoke of the success of our FOND-dews and the publication of Peter Trudgill's new book, *The Norfolk Dialect*, as being the highlights of his first year in office as chairman.

Also in this winter 2003 edition of the *Mawkin* was a reflective, appreciative article about the dialect seminars by **Anna McCarthy**, Arts in Education Project Development Officer, Norfolk County Council, enthusing on the success of the event:

Dialect seminars' big success

We were delighted, after months of planning and preparation, finally to be able to bring to teachers this INSET opportunity designed to develop their knowledge of language development and to learn about the influence of regional accents and dialects.

Norfolk County Council's Arts in Education and Literacy teams worked together with the tireless FOND to bring the inspirational Professor Peter Trudgill and Dr Ken Lodge to our county's teachers, who came from schools, the Traveller Education Service, the English Language Support Service and advisers from Norfolk Education Advisory Services.

BBC Radio Norfolk was also in attendance to record live interviews, and there was a great deal of interest from the wider community too! The innovative partnership project has elicited the following responses:

"This is the most interesting course I have been on in eight years in the county. I would be interested in any related or follow-up session." "This has taught me to celebrate diversity in language." "Thank you for a fascinating day!"

We learned not only about language development, but came away with a much stronger sense of the identity of Norfolk itself, and are looking forward very much to developing this work further.

Thank you, Norman, thank you, Peter!

The future was looking good for one of FOND's dearest aims — to introduce an understanding and appreciation of Norfolk dialect into local schools' curricula. To this end, *The Merry Mawkin* reported in the spring of 2004 that 'much activity behind the scenes' was continuing at county level.

CHAPTER 18

Recording delight

MEANWHILE, on the recording front, our technical adviser, **Stewart Orr**, had written in the winter of 2003:

> In the autumn edition of *The Merry Mawkin* I reported on a day's briefing for recordists at Prior's Croft Barn, Withersdale. Now for the results of the briefing.
>
> I've just been processing some of the work that has come in, and it's been a total delight! Recordings made by FOND members Jean Eaglen and Mike Coley are crisp and clear — exactly what we need for our embryonic archive.
>
> For each person recorded I receive a mini-disc. This is the unedited production, which I copy to a CD. I make sure the CD tracks are not longer than about 10 minutes each, to help the listener find his way about the disc easily.
>
> CDs are then made for our own archive, for the Norfolk Record Office and a working copy for our newly-appointed archivist, Anne Doggett, to log and index.
>
> To some extent we are still feeling our way towards organising a regular system and these first few recordings are helping to sort this out. When they have been copied, logged and archived, further copies will be made, so recordist and interviewee will have access to them.
>
> Working copies will be held by the committee, and will be available to any member who likes to book them out.

Early in 2004 Stewart Orr announced: "It is gratifying to report that we are steadily building up a team of interviewers around the county with master tapes being lodged with the new Norfolk Record Office recently opened by the Queen."

One of this team, committee member **Jean Eaglen**, of Hingham, reported:

> "I would like to encourage any member of FOND to 'have a go' at the recording of our dialect, whilst meeting some really interesting people along the way.
>
> "I've learnt an awful lot of stories that happened in my childhood, along with memories of catching bishy barny-bees (ladybirds) in jam jars and having dodman (snail) races, with a spare lettuce leaf being used as a lure."

Jean said she had spent many a happy hour recording, with laughter a constant ingredient. "I'm always happy to pass on my experience to anyone in the Hingham area who would like to take up the challenge and try their hand at this very worthwhile activity of preserving our dialect and memories for future generations to enjoy," she added.

Two other FOND highlights in 2004.

Lead story in the summer edition of the *Mawkin* proclaimed:

FOND's festival foray

FOND's first joint venture with a town festival was judged a success when the Harleston Festival organising committee invited us to join their celebrations.

With our education officer Norman Hart acting as the catalyst, we sponsored a dialect writing competition with the active co-operation of the town's C of E VA Primary School.

Pupils in the under-7 and 7–11 age groups were invited to submit their original stories under the title 'Dew yu write us a good owd tale', with book tokens to the value of £50 on offer as prizes; half-sponsored by FOND and with the other half generously provided by Norman.

The winners in each category were Rhian Earrye and Isobel Cockle, who read their winning entries to an audience of some 80 people in the town's Apollo Rooms.

The evening continued with an archive film with the theme of Food and Drink in the Waveney Valley and ended with a Spin-Off Theatre production of *Lion Heart*, the epic tale of the hero Roland as he takes on the Herculean tasks of battling his way round the Norfolk Broads in a leaky inflatable rubber duck in search of his one true love.

Directed by Eve Stebbing and told by Paul Preston Mills, it was full of audience participation and ideal for those looking for something new in story telling, or, as one member of the audience commented: 'I've never seen anything like that before!' "

Lead story in the *Mawkin's* autumn edition, 2004:

FOND at the Forum

Through the good offices of our education officer Norman Hart, FOND was invited to provide a display at the recent *Discover Your Heritage* ten-day promotion at the Forum in Norwich.

The invitation included the provision of three display panels, a table and the offer of administrative back-up, all free of charge so that we could promote FOND, its activities, membership and aspirations.

Our thanks are due to Sheridan Smith, marketing manager to the Forum Trust, for all her help and support.

We displayed promotional material on every aspect of FOND activities, along with membership forms and a competition devised by Norman and FOND chairman Peter Brooks.

"As the first exercise of its kind for us," wrote Peter, "we learned a lot on how to improve our presentations, met a wide range of interesting people, gave out membership forms (enrolling some new members 'on the spot'), discovered some new dialect words and generally promoted our society in a positive way.

"It is hoped that we will be able to provide FOND's appearance at other venues in the future."

CHAPTER 19

The Singing Postman

NO BOOK ABOUT NORFOLK and its dialect would be complete without paying homage to **Allan Smethurst**, the Singing Postman, who did so much to keep the county's precious identity alive.

Keith Skipper, in his book *Hev Yew Gotta Loight, Boy?*, published by Countryside Books in 2001, wrote: "Allan Smethurst, in the guise of the Singing Postman, burst into the pop charts and also the affections of the nation in 1965 with his great hit *Hev Yew Gotta Loight, Boy*?

"His songs had been charming people in Norfolk for a while before that, recalling the events of his boyhood and the places he had known. They were put across to the strum of his guitar, with a cheery but plaintive delivery that connected immediately with his audiences.

"His 1965 hit brought a celebrity status that swept him along. There were concerts galore, fetes to open, a summer booking at Great Yarmouth, and he was mobbed by fans outside the Co-op in Stowmarket. But it was not a role he could sustain. Allan was at his most brilliant at small gatherings, ideally inside a cosy pub, with a buxom barmaid, a game of dummies on the table, and the chatter of heady local appreciation.

"After a few brief years in the spotlight, he spent much of the rest of his life as a recluse in a Salvation Army hostel in Grimsby, where he died in December, 2000. Sadly, this was just as there began to be an increasing interest in his work, and the reissue of his recordings on CDs in 2001.

"Allan Smethurst was born in Bury, Lancashire, in 1927. He came to Norfolk at the age of two when his family moved to Sheringham and his fond childhood memories served to inspire many songs from a prolific pen as his career blossomed. He had started to sift through nostalgic snapshots as a teenager when his invalid father died, his Norfolk-born mother remarried and the family headed for Cleethorpes.

Allan Smethurst, the Singing Postman.

Keith Skipper continued: "Lyrics soaked in affection for the county he missed so much stood out clearly as he abandoned efforts to be an electrician and put on the postman's uniform which was destined to bring him a remarkable round as a national celebrity.

"That round all but ended in 1970 after a few brief years in the spotlight and he spent much of the rest of his life as a virtual recluse in the Grimsby hostel.

"Sadly, Allan found it difficult to cope with the pressures of stardom. Perhaps his backers and handlers should have done better, although showbiz momentum is mighty hard to hold in check once it's on a roll.

"Whatever verdicts we pin on the Singing Postman's brief tilt at show business – and he did outsell the Beatles for a spell, at least in East Anglia – he deserves much more than the cheery nod often reserved for passing novelty acts."

At one of our FOND-dews, at Martham Village Hall in June, 2001, a fascinating insight into the life and songs of Allan Smethurst was provided by Tony Palmer, of Anglian Music at Caister. Tony worked very hard in the 1970s in a bid to revive Allan's recording career and later issued a selection of seven CDs featuring all the Singing Postman songs.

In November, 2007, a tribute evening in honour of Norfolk's most unlikely pop star was held in the Harbour Room at Blakeney just after what would have been Allan's 80th birthday.

CHAPTER 20

Ted Ellis and Rex Hancy

WHILE *The Merry Mawkin* is responsible for keeping FOND members aware of the progress being made with the preservation and proclamation of the Norfolk dialect, elsewhere within its pages were to be found a variety of features, not least the writings of **Ted Ellis**.

One of Norfolk's best known naturalists and broadcasters, Ted Ellis, who died in 1986, aged 77, was born in Guernsey of Norfolk parents. From 1928 to 1956 he was Keeper of Natural History at Norwich Castle Museum, but living with his family in a remote cottage at Wheatfen Broad, Surlingham, among 130 acres of woodland and fen close to the River Yare, five miles east of Norwich.

Ted Ellis: naturalist, broadcaster and gifted essayist. Drawing by David Poole.

A skilled writer, for some 35 years Ted wrote a daily essay for the *Eastern Daily Press* and a fortnightly article in *The Guardian* and in 1982 many of these articles were published in *Ted Ellis's Countryside Reflections*, a book superbly illustrated with evocative drawings by David Poole.

Former *Eastern Daily Press* literary and arts editor Charles Roberts wrote at the time about Ted Ellis: "His writing was, and is, crafted with the lyricism of an essayist. It lives within its own time-shell – and yet it is timeless. For what he saw and communicated has its own continuum. He revealed to us a life force which, with fierce patience born of millennia of natural rhythm, holds out despite all the depredations of man."

Since his death in 1986, Wheatfen Broad, under the guidance of his widow, the late Phyllis, has become a permanent nature reserve, through the Ted Ellis Trust.

In 2001, after a visit to Wheatfen with some ex-*EDP* colleagues and a privileged conducted tour by Phyllis, she kindly gave me permission to publish any of Ted's essays in *The Merry Mawkin*, and from the autumn edition, No 4, they became a regular feature throughout my editorship.

Here are three examples of the beautifully crafted writing of Ted Ellis:

Dawn of a new day

Surlingham, June 21st, 1970

Either the warmth of the night or the loud pealing of a thrush's notes woke me at three o'clock in time to set forth into the fragrance and mystery of a midsummer dawn.

Moon daisies shone in the tall grass, though dewy clover leaves were still folded in sleep. The air was filled with gossamer, and mosquitoes zoomed at me from every quarter. Glow-worm lamps had faded, and a white ground mist lay over the fen, with spikes of iris and flowering grasses pricking through it in silhouette.

Small bats whisked round the trees in a final spurt of excitement before retiring to their crevices and they dived at me like the angry terns of Blakeney, squeaking explosively in my face for a fraction of a second.

While the bird chorus rose to a crescendo in the nearby woods, and shrilling wrens whirred out of the undergrowth, sedge-warblers churred and chattered in the reeds, and first one and, presently, three cuckoos began calling. One was in perfect tune, the second doubled its lower note and the third was sadly flat and faultering.

A cock crowed up in the village, but there were no echoes from pheasants at their roost just then, although I could hear some conversational greylags stirring on the broad.

Strangely enough, song thrushes dominated the woodland chorus, while the half light lingered, and it was not until ten minutes past four that the first blackbird joined in (by no means ecstatically) and it was then, also, that I heard the first bumble bee buzzing round a patch of comfrey.

Colour flooded back gently into flowers everywhere now; the yellow irises in the fen, pink ragged robin, valerian and dog rose and lordly foxgloves, half in woodland shade.

The last pale moths zigzagged into hiding and another golden day had arrived.

Summer Evening

Surlingham, July 14th, 1950

As I look out of the window this evening, the mellow gold of late sunshine streaks the grass softly and filters between the trees of the oak wood across the way. A white admiral butterfly toys with the high-climbing honeysuckle; a dappled, illusive creature of fairyland. From an oak on the sunny side a solitary thrush is pouring forth a surprisingly sweet little song and a ring dove coos contentedly in any ivy bower.

But silence reigns among the crowds of chaffinches; the shrill wrens and plaintive robins are dumb. Even the nightingale is a changeling now, uttering only harsh curses and warning spitfire cracks of sound from bushes when he is disturbed.

All those silvery whisperings and tremulous voices of the small warblers are missing now. The grasshoppers make dry jiffling sounds underfoot instead; and the solemn zooming of a hornet becomes majestic music in the woods.

When night falls, I know that no mewing of owls will break the spell and I shall hear only that faint singing of my own pulses when I stand under the starlit sky and try to imagine, like the ancients, that it is the music of the spheres that floats down through the silence.

Drawing by David Poole, from Ted Ellis's Countryside Reflections, 1953.

Reindeer Moon

The moss is silvered in the glade
This gentle night
And ferns like phantom wreaths are laid
In secret light.
A reindeer moon rides in the sky
And crystal frost
Crisps leaves to tinsel as they lie
On paths embossed
With patterns of a travelled way.
Aside, I see
Pricked out with stars unknown to day,
A holly tree;
Its berries mutely flushed with peace.
An ivy cloak
Steals radiance of a golden fleece
From gilded oak
And from its folds a weird flute
Wavers away –
A brown owl's tremulous salute
And solemn say.
Great trees tonight a cloister make
And standing here
Beneath the reindeer moon, I take
Thought of the year.

Ted Ellis died on July 22, 1986, after a lifetime devoted to natural history. The *Eastern Daily Press* was then faced with the task of finding a successor to undertake the nature commentaries Ted had provided in every *EDP* for 35 years.

The problem was solved by obtaining the services of four local naturalists, each one contributing to *In the Countryside* for one week every month. One of them was **Rex Hancy**, naturalist and former teacher and vice-president of the Norfolk and Norwich Naturalists' Society.

An old schoolfriend of mine in the Waveney Valley, Rex contributed this article for the winter 2003 edition of *The Merry Mawkin*:

A memory of wartime by the Waveney

September 3rd, 1939. A few days before my tenth birthday. We had sat in fearful silence listening to our crackling wireless as Neville Chamberlain spelled out the dire fact that we were at war with Germany.

A minute after the fearful announcement, I was planning how I could best stem the advance of enemy troops. They would surely be upon us, if not by the end of the day at least by teatime tomorrow.

My 'country', a few square miles of our beloved Waveney Valley, was worth defending. For all the trials and hardship of pre-war life we were fiercely proud of our home.

Beyond the nearby villages were other complexes, even small towns and, too huge to imagine, 'The City'. All were inhabited by strange folk who spoke our language but in peculiar forms.

The newspapers told me of conflicts in the greater world from China, Africa

Rex Hancy: one of Ted Ellis's successors in the EDP's In the Countryside.

and countries much nearer home. All gave cause for apprehension.

Mind you, I knew how to conduct myself. We owned a tattered volume of *The Boys' Own Paper* from 1907. When minor ailments kept me from school I mined its treasures – things to make and do, exciting adventure stories.

Boys were sent off to boarding school where they learned to say much in few words. They discovered how to behave in difficult and dangerous circumstances, to fight on with rigidly stiff upper lip with only a faithful native servant beside them.

The grey army did not arrive on our doorstep. The only excitement was the deployment of a searchlight battery consisting of one light and a set of enormous earphones. The men were Territorials from London. London was not exactly a foreign land, but they were the first of men from all over the world we were soon to meet. School carried on as usual, apart from one inconvenience. When air raid warnings sounded we had to sit under our desks. Enormous fun for five minutes! After that we became bored and naughty.

Then came my big idea. Why not carry on work until an actual aeroplane could be heard? I volunteered to patrol outside all by myself, missing lessons and feeling smugly important. The next time the warning sounded, I moved to resume official duties. "No, Rex, you've been out before. We'll send someone else."

What a let-down! Soon the system was abandoned and we worked on, secure in the knowledge our dads had pasted strips of paper over all the window panes!

Rex Hancy was honorary president of Norfolk and Norwich Naturalists' Society for the one-year term 1986–87 and chairman 1994 to 1997, when he was appointed perpetual vice-president. He has been East Anglian representative of the British Plant Gall Society since it was launched in 1985 and was chairman from 1999 to 2002 and in 2004 he was made an honorary life member. Rex and his wife Barbara, who shares his enthusiasm for and expertise in natural history, were awarded the Sydney Long Memorial Medal in 2007 'for a significant contribution to natural history in Norfolk and beyond'.

CHAPTER 21

Sidney Grapes

KEITH SKIPPER HAS DESCRIBED **Sidney Grapes** as the most endearing of local characters. The forerunner many years earlier of Tony Clarke's Boy Jimma, Sidney came to county fame as a rustic comedian at local concerts and dinners. He will be most fondly remembered, however, for 'The Boy John Letters' he wrote to the *Eastern Daily Press* from 1946 until his death in 1958.

He lived all his life in the Broadland village of Potter Heigham, where he ran a garage business. The Boy John Letters, says Keith, were a delightful microcosm of village life, written in dialect but never swamped by it. They were composed by a countryman who wrote as he spoke and spelt as he pleased. He happily combined written and stage entertainments in an appealing and enduring style.

PICTURE: JOHN SEYMOUR, NORWICH

The Boy John: as epitomised by Sidney Grapes

The letters featured The Boy John, Granfar, Aunt Agatha and the scandalous Oul Mrs W—. "Perhaps the letters were more eagerly anticipated because they were infrequent. Sidney was pressed to become a regular weekly contributor, but he was as wary of the blandishments of journalism as he was of the professional stage," wrote Keith in his book, *The Norfolk Connection*, published in 1991.

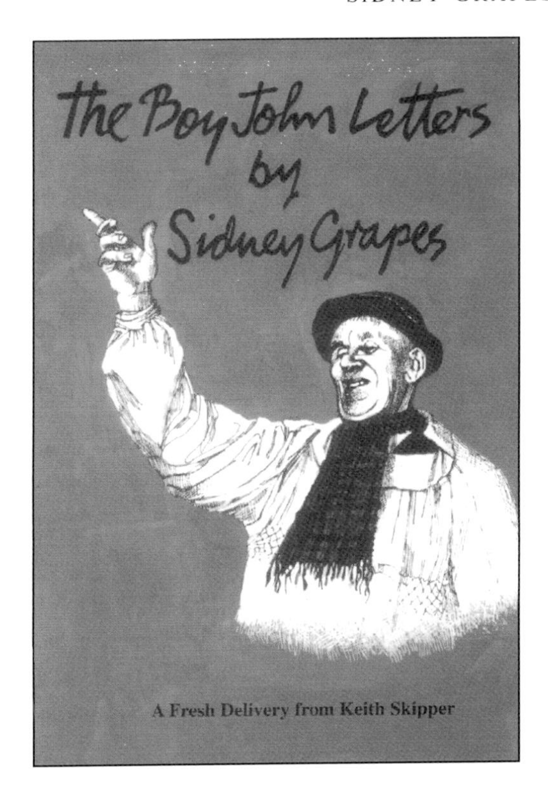

Sidney Grapes: the front cover of The Boy John Letters – A Fresh Delivery from Keith Skipper, Mousehold Press 2003.

Many readers 'cheated' and always went to the P.S. for Aunt Agatha's latest example of homespun philosophy – P.S. Aunt Agatha she say, 'The more you say, the less people remember'.

An endearing tribute to Sidney's special skills came from a former Bishop of Norwich, the Rt Rev Percy Herbert, speaking at the Potter Heigham Church dedication service on November 23, 1958.

"It is not given to many writers to create fictitious characters that are so alive, and that once met will never be forgotten," said the Bishop. "To read those letters is really to be enriched and then to go on our way with the new courage that they breathe all the time, and a new joy in our hearts that we should be alive…

"He was not only an astonishingly fine natural humorist, he was an incomparable teller of good stories."

The Merry Mawkin's winter edition of 2003 included a review of Keith's new book, *The Boy John Letters, by Sidney Grapes – A Fresh Delivery from Keith Skipper.*

The letters were back in circulation by popular demand, adding a fresh appreciation of them. Skip had also recorded a companion CD with Sheilah Olley as Aunt Agatha, introduced by Adrian Bell, of publisher Mousehold Press.

PICTURE: CANON PETER NICHOLSON

Sidney Grapes and his wife, Ella, outside their shop in Potter Heigham.

On March 30, 2008, a special tribute to Sidney Grapes was paid in the form of a FOND-dew organised by John Austrin in the Village Hall at Potter Heigham, home territory of John and, of course, Sidney.

There were readings of Sidney's works from Owen Church, Norah Brindid, Elizabeth Austrin (the Gal Liza of the Press Gang), Pat Munday, Mervin Hinton, Pat Maitland and John Beck. John had driven from Benfleet in Essex for the occasion and gave a virtuoso performance of *The Washerwoman*, by Sidney the songwriter.

An oft-repeated local recollection is of the notice that Sidney put up at his Potter Heigham garage just before the festive season:

"A Happy Christmas to all my customers wot hev paid their bills, and a prosperous New Year to them wot hent."

CHAPTER 22

Dick Bagnall-Oakeley

ONE OF THE JOBS of a district reporter on a local newspaper in the 1950s was to attend funerals and take the names of the 'others present' as they entered church. I was standing in the porch of West Runton Parish Church before the funeral of a well-known member of the community when a familiar figure approached and proffered his name to me: "R P Bagnall-Oakeley".

As I entered it into my notebook, I checked the spelling of Oakeley, emphasising the extra 'e' (the more common spelling, of course, being Oakley). He seemed surprised and pleased I'd got it right, no doubt having seen it miss-spelt many times in the past!

Dick Bagnall-Oakeley was a Norfolk dialect expert and naturalist and taught geography at Gresham's School, Holt. His early years were spent at Hemsby, where his father was vicar. He was educated at Gresham's and Clare College, Cambridge, and at the age of 25 was asked to 'hold the fort for a fortnight' as a geography teacher at Gresham's, and remained there for the rest of his long teaching career.

Dick Bagnall-Oakeley: teacher, dialect expert and naturalist.

"His skills were abundant and varied," writes Keith Skipper in his 1991 book, *The Norfolk Connection*, "and he represented the county at hockey, athletics and rifle shooting. But from childhood, natural history, ornithology in particular, was his first love."

"He made himself an authority on migrant birds in north Norfolk, and he was an expert on capturing all wildlife and plant life on film. His informative yet humorous talks about natural history, both on local television programmes and at lectures throughout the region, made him a well-known figure.

"Often he would break into the Norfolk dialect, which he loved and at which he was an expert. He feared it was disappearing as an older generation died and parts of their vocabulary were lost. He also wrote about natural history in numerous articles and in books, and he was invited to lecture throughout Britain and abroad."

Tragically, Mr Bagnall-Oakeley collapsed and died at the wheel of his car in April, 1974, aged 66, while driving to Inverness, where he was to have given a lecture on ornithology.

In Edition 8 of *The Merry Mawkin*, we carried a story in which the writings of the late Dick Bagnall-Oakeley played an important part. FOND's website co-ordinator Pauline Dodd had received the following e-mail:

> "My grandfather, Albert Redling, sadly died this week, aged 98. All his life Norfolk was his spiritual home, though he died in Hertfordshire.
>
> "Each year, since he was a boy, he would visit his family in Methwold Hythe for his holidays. He was never happier than in rural Norfolk. His pace, his humour and even his way of talking felt rooted there.
>
> "I am reading a tribute at his funeral on Friday and I wondered if any of your members had any suggestions for a suitable short reading that might capture the spirit of Norfolk that he so loved.
>
> "I was prompted to call you after hearing Stephen Fry's broadcast about Norfolk dialect on Radio 4 the night before my grandfather died."

The writer's name was Jeremy Williams and his request galvanised Pauline and FOND into immediate action!

Into Pauline's mind, reported the *Mawkin*, came a piece of prose written by Dick Bagnall-Oakeley, which begins: *Norfolk is not simply a word that describes a county. Norfolk describes also a language, a humour and a way of life...*

After receiving a phone call from Pauline, I contacted Keith Skipper for permission to use the essay from which that quote came and which appeared in Skip's 1994 book, *The Norfolk Companion*, and this is it:

> "*Norfolk* is not simply a word that describes a county. *Norfolk* describes also a language, a humour and a way of life.
>
> "Spoken Norfolk has a stout and uniquely resistant quality and only people born in the county are able properly to penetrate it and repeat it with their own tongues.
>
> "Just as their language, so also the people of Norfolk are tough, resistant and impenetrable. They guard to themselves the secrets of their language and of their humour.
>
> "Yet humour there is in the Norfolk people, riotous and abundant.
>
> "When you read Norfolk tales, remember that they are tales about a highly observant, subtle and recondite people. Therefore, always think twice before you laugh at a Norfolk tale – the laugh might be on you."

The words of the master were duly read at Albert Redling's funeral and a delighted Jeremy Williams later reported to Pauline that, thanks to FOND, his grandfather's wishes had been fulfilled.

Earlier in this book, in Chapter 12, Baroness Gillian Shephard quoted briefly a Bagnall-Oakeley example of Norfolk brevity. It bears relating in full!

Mr Bagnall-Oakeley had written:

> In the winter of 1963 I was making a film on the changes of habit imposed upon seabirds by prolonged exposure to hunger and severe cold. I chose a spot on the coast near Salthouse as the

ideal view for a long background shot upon which the credits for the film could be superimposed.

I arrived a little early on a bitter evening in February with the temperature reading eight degrees of frost and I stood in the lee of a small cliff for the sun to sink to the right angle.

One other person went down to the cold, desolate stretch of coastline that evening. He was an old beachcomber, raggedly but warmly dressed, wheeling his bicycle with him on the off-chance that a plank might be there among the driftwood washed up by the freezing tide.

For about 20 minutes I stood in such shelter as the cliff provided, but the sun still had not descended to the angle I wanted before the beachcomber had completed his tour and started to return.

He passed me, still standing in eight degrees of frost, immobile in the same position as I had been in when he passed before.

This time he spoke as he passed, and in the one word he uttered I heard all the plain speech, the avoidance of the play of 'polite' conversation, the laconic brevity and the shrewd humour that I have come to know and love in Norfolk people.

Not a shabby, anonymous beachcomber, he summed himself up in an expression echoing all the ironic humour and the unanswerable understatement of a true Norfolk character:

"Sweatin'? "

CHAPTER 23

Major milestone

NEWS OF A MAJOR MILESTONE in the history of FOND appeared in the 2005 spring edition of *The Merry Mawkin* when chairman **Peter Brooks** announced in the front page lead story:

We're on our way – and all set for FOND's educational initiative

As members will know, it has long been a main objective to get an understanding and appreciation of our dialect into Norfolk's schools. Not to persuade children to include dialect in their everyday speech, but to gain an insight into how our language has developed and adapted over the years and the part that dialect has played in the process.

Now, after many months of consultations, research, establishing a programme and submitting an extremely detailed application, the way forward looks good – thanks to a £24,600 grant from the Local Heritage Initiative fund.

£1. Free to FOND members

Spring 2005 No 17

The Merry Mawkin

Newsletter of Friends of Norfolk Dialect

Chairman Reports: "We're on our way — and all set for FOND's Educational Initiative"

As members will know, it has long been a main objective to get an understanding and appreciation of our dialect into Norfolk's schools. Not to persuade children to include dialect in their everyday speech, but to gain an insight into how our language has developed and adapted over the years and the part that dialect has played in the process.

Now, after many months of consultations, research, establishing a programme and submitting an extremely detailed application, the way forward looks good — thanks to a £24,600 grant from the Local Heritage Initiative fund.

The three year project will involve a close working partnership with the Norfolk County Council Education Advisory Service and, through them, with ten schools and their communities across the county of Norfolk.

It promises to be an interesting and challenging initiative which we look forward to with determination and enthusiasm, and I hope you will agree that the project title of **FONDLY NORFOLK** is an appropriate one!

A Promise, Punk rock and Buckingham Palace

Norfolk dialect has been in the news since our last newsletter. From a promise by the BBC, to a punk rock band and the elegance of Buckingham Palace.

In January the BBC launched its ***Voices*** project, a nationwide survey involving interviews with people across the UK with the aim of creating an online interactive dialect map of the British Isles. Five members of FOND were invited to a recording session at Radio Norfolk's Norwich studio to record, and talk about, our native dialect.

"We're on our way!": The Merry Mawkin, spring 2005

> The three-year project will involve a close working partnership with the Norfolk County Council Education Advisory Service and, through them, with ten schools and their communities across the county of Norfolk.
>
> It promises to be an interesting and challenging initiative which we look forward to with determination and enthusiasm, and I hope you will agree that the project title of 'Fondly Norfolk' is an appropriate one!

In the 2005 autumn edition of the *Mawkin*, Peter Brooks reported that ten schools across the county had been identified as being willing to be included in a programme of community events. Dates had been allocated for training days, a county-based exhibition and other activities.

The project had been made possible by the £24,600 grant from the combined support of the Local Heritage Initiative, the Heritage Lottery Fund, the Nationwide Building Society and the Countryside Agency.

> "It is a partnership," wrote Peter, "between FOND and the Children's Services Department of the Norfolk County Council and in its wider context aims to raise awareness of the origins, history, development and current use and richness of the Norfolk dialect as a local cultural heritage asset by various means, including collecting and archiving recording, exhibitions, events, seminars, publications and other initiatives."

The chairman also reported that FOND's first recording of Norfolk dialect and reminiscences, many from the older generation, were now on sale.

The recordings were unedited versions of the interviews with the intention that in due course all would be edited under 'theme' subjects, such as farming, family life and fishing.

Master copies of the thirteen recordings made by our team of interviewers had been deposited with the Norfolk Sound Archive.

By the spring of 2006 the number of Norfolk schools taking part in the project, called *Lost in Translation: An Exploration of the Norfolk Dialect*, had risen to eleven and they were listed in the *Mawkin* as:

Brancaster Primary; Diss High; Firside Middle, Hellesdon; Forncett St Peter C of E; Great Ryburgh All Saints Primary; Harleston C of E Primary; Hewett, Norwich; Langham Primary; Sheringham Primary; Thompson Primary; and Wymondham High.

FOND technical adviser Stewart Orr wrote:

> "*Lost in Translation* has seen the acquisition of ten sets of recording gear suitable for teachers and schoolchildren to go out into the field to record Norfolk dialect.
>
> "After *Lost in Translation* has run its course, there will be ten sets of equipment, either for us at FOND or for other organisations with similar interests to use.
>
> "With each of the eleven schools producing twenty recordings, we will end up with some 200 additions to the archive.
>
> "This is something both we at FOND and Jonathan Draper, the sound man at the Norfolk Archive Centre, look forward to with keen anticipation."

The Queen with Dr John Alban, county archivist, after she had officially opened the Archive Centre at Norfolk Record Office, County Hall, on February 5, 2004.

CHAPTER 24

Third chairman hits out

THREE YEARS HAD ELAPSED since Peter Brooks succeeded Keith Skipper as chairman of FOND and now, under the society's constitution, it was time for a successor to take over.

Tony Clarke, vice-chairman since October, 2002, was duly elected to the chairmanship at the 2005 AGM at the Lincoln Hall, Hingham, on November 27.

And it was a hard-hitting speech that the new chairman delivered that afternoon, far removed from Tony's yokel Boy Jimma of stage and page fame, as reported in the winter 2005 edition of the *Mawkin*:

'A lot of ill-informed prejudice to overcome'

I think what we all have to remember is that we are not here simply to try to breathe life into something which is virtually extinct. What we are trying to do is to conserve an important part of our heritage and encourage society at large to give it the respect it deserves.

In this endeavour we still have a lot of ill-informed prejudice to overcome.

Yet, if some developer came along and proposed converting Norwich Castle into a block of flats or demolishing the Cathedral, or the Custom House at King's Lynn, or Blickling Hall, on the grounds that they are too expensive to maintain, there would, quite naturally, be an outcry.

Those are spectacular, visible pieces of our heritage. Projects such as the award-winning Time and Tide Museum at Yarmouth are cropping up all over the place to arouse interest in the way of life of our ancestors. Why, therefore, should we sit back and allow the language they spoke simply to disintegrate without trace?

There is a danger in groups such as FOND, that we become too parochial, preserving a manner of speech simply for reasons of nostalgia. We need to broaden the debate on dialect while, at the same time, remaining realistic as to the limitations of what we can achieve.

The fact is that, in this country, there are fashionable accents, usually the urban ones, and unfashionable accents, which are more often the rural ones.

Ours, unfortunately, comes under the latter heading. Frankly, the most difficult job we face, even in our own county, is to be taken seriously.

Now you may think this comment is odd coming from a bloke who is best known for appearing on stage as a country yokel called The Boy Jimma. Well, we are our own worst enemies, because the traditional Norfolk style of humour is not to take the mickey out of other people but to poke gentle fun at ourselves.

Tony Clarke: 'Encourage society to give our heritage the respect it deserves.'.

We are past masters at the in-joke, which is why traditional Norfolk comedians don't make the big time on TV and radio.

I know you will tell me that there is a subtle difference between dialect and accent, and there is, but unfortunately they are related.

We have to accept that in this age of multi-channel radio, TV, the internet and text messaging, regional accents are the dying embers of regional languages which should be recorded because they hold up a mirror to the history of England.

They contained a mixture of words which either grew up in those various regions or were introduced, through the centuries, by immigrants from other countries.

The Norfolk Dialect, by Peter Trudgill – in Poppyland Publishing's 'Norfolk Origins' series, 2003.

What is serious, however, is that over the years our younger generation has been made to feel ashamed of its accent. There was a case, earlier this year, of a Norfolk band who had been told by music producers that they would never top the charts unless they changed their accents.

And when I went to have a haircut the other day the hairdresser said he had had some youngsters in who tried to talk like Londoners (heaven forbid!), because it was more cool than their 'mother tongue'.

We also have to bear in mind that all languages – except Latin, perhaps – continue to change through the generations. In the 16th century the first language of 37 per cent of the inhabitants of Norwich was Dutch or French, rather than English (I'm quoting here from Peter Trudgill's book on *The Norfolk Dialect*). In Nelson's day everybody, even admirals, spoke with a regional accent. There was no such thing as 'posh talk', or even standard English.

Then the Victorians started to tidy it all up, and create a standard English language. Today, having given our national language to a large slice of the world, we are now dismantling it to the point where it is changing, probably at a faster rate than ever before. This is partly because a generation of young people has grown up never having been taught the fascinating subtleties of grammar, or even the true meaning of words. Have you noticed how the entire human race is being dehumanised by the disappearance of the word 'who'? We are always hearing on TV about 'people that' do something. Or that people from other countries are 'different to' us rather than 'different from'.

And did you notice what I thought was the silliest offence committed against the English language by the media around the season of Remembrance?

We were solemnly informed that the lives of the few remaining survivors of the first world war – all aged between 100 and 109 – had 'spanned three centuries'! That would have made them more than 300 years old. Their lives, of course, had *touched* three centuries, which is a remarkable enough achievement anyway. A bridge which spans only one-third of a river is no use to anybody.

England was once a rich tapestry of interlocking regional accents, a bit like a linguistic jigsaw puzzle. But you may wonder what chance we have of conserving our regional accents if, as a nation, we can't even protect our national language?

Well, FOND's schools project is a start, even though it is difficult for we laymen to find our way through the labyrinth of bureaucratic language employed by the educationalised (*jargon*). But we can't leave it at that. People of all ages, but especially young people, need somehow to be persuaded to be proud of their accent rather than ashamed of it, because it is part of their heritage.

Perhaps we can start by having an exchange of views in the *Mawkin*. Maybe we can ask members, through our newsletter, to put forward their own ideas on dialect and what FOND should be doing to promote it.

Maybe we need new ideas for our social 'dews' around the county with greater involvement from the members. Rather than simply inviting a speaker, perhaps we could have quizzes with teams from different areas of the county invited to compete against each other.

Maybe, for one 'dew', we could have a competition to see who can construct the best *Mawkin*? Perhaps this would introduce a bit more fun into our serious subject.

Perhaps we can broaden our horizons by reaching out to dialect groups in other regions of England, trying to find out how they operate and exchanging ideas with them.

Tony's thought-provoking address raised many questions at the meeting and seemed to have struck a chord with members.

Sadly, as described in Chapter 1, because of ill-health, Tony Clarke was able to complete only one year as chairman and after a three-year battle with cancer, he died in November, 2008.

Tony was succeeded in 2006 by Colin Burleigh (as will be related in Chapter 35).

Incidentally, Tony's dream of 'reaching out to dialect groups in other regions of England' began to come true in 2006 when links were forged and exchange visits arranged between FOND and the East Lincolnshire Dialect Society (more details to follow in Chapter 33).

CHAPTER 25

Bryan Gunn at home in Norfolk

IT WAS IN THE WINTER 2005 edition of *The Merry Mawkin* – the last to be produced by caretaker-editor Peter Brooks – that Norwich City Football Club's **Bryan Gunn** made an appearance in the 'Norfolk by Adoption' series.

The Canaries' former goalkeeper succeeded Glenn Roeder as manager for seven months in 2009, but several years earlier, through his unstinting charitable work, he had already become highly respected in the community, culminating with his appointment as Sheriff of Norwich.

Bryan Gunn, Norwich City FC manager in 2009, had already held high office in the community, having been Sheriff of Norwich in 2002–2003.

Peter Brooks wrote in the *Mawkin*:

> Bryan Gunn was born in Thurso, Caithness, in 1963. He joined Aberdeen FC at 14 and within two years had signed a two-year contract to play in the reserves. At 18 he became goalkeeper in the first team. His manager was a gentleman by the name of Alex Ferguson.

After the death of their daughter in 1992, Bryan and his wife Susan launched their leukaemia appeal which, amongst other things, established the Francesca Gunn Laboratory at the UEA, where this picture was taken.

Bryan came to Norfolk in 1986 as goalkeeper for Norwich City. He made 477 first team appearances in the next 12 years and was twice voted Norwich City Player of the Year.

So what attracted him south of the border? Former City goalkeeper Chris Woods had moved to Rangers and Bryan came to Norwich with a recommendation from Sir Alex.

Bryan returned briefly to Scotland to play for Hibernian, but after a broken leg he returned to Norwich as the club's new sponsorship sales manager and community ambassador, and in February, 2007, moved back into football as club liaison for the Canaries.

In his career he won six caps for Scotland, four of which were in World Cup qualifiers in 1993.

Bryan, wrote Peter Brooks in the *Mawkin*, gives the impression of having settled naturally into Norfolk life and sees little difference between his native Scottish friends and family and the friends he has made here, although he thinks those north of the border may be a little more 'firey'. As far as the local accent is concerned, he finds broad Norfolk sometimes difficult to follow.

He said that since he came to Norwich the city had changed, with many more entertainment and night-life opportunities but, overall, he believes life in the county offers a safe environment – 'a nice place for children to grow up in'.

With his family he enjoys days at the coast, finds plenty of places to take the dogs for a walk and has a special affection for country pubs. He is convinced we enjoy a better, calmer, climate than other UK regions, but thinks we have some of the worst roads in the country!

After the death of their two-year-old daughter Francesca in 1992, Bryan and his wife Susan launched their leukaemia appeal, which, by 2005, had already raised over £800,000, established a Francesca Gunn Laboratory at the UEA, paid for nursing sisters at hospitals in Norwich and Gorleston and launched a support line for parents of children with cancer or leukaemia.

Bryan's appointment as Sheriff of Norwich for 2002–2003 confirmed his acceptance by the citizens of the city in the year of the Canaries' centenary season and the granting of the Freedom of the City to the football club, and the tenth anniversary of the Bryan Gunn Leukaemia Appeal.

Susan has achieved international acclaim in the arts world since gaining a first-class BA honours degree in fine art at Norwich School of Art and Design.

CHAPTER 26

Queen 'slips into Norfolk dialect'

According to Princess Michael of Kent, in an interview with a German newspaper, the Queen enjoys slipping into Norfolk dialect during family gatherings.

Learning of this, **Peter Brooks**, in his third and final year as FOND chairman, decided to write to Her Majesty. "It seemed too good an opportunity to miss," reported Peter in the winter 2005 edition of *The Merry Mawkin*. "So I wrote to HM, enclosing a copy of Keith Skipper's book *Larn Yarself Norfolk* and informing her she was a 'Good ow' gal' – the ultimate Norfolk compliment!

"The result was a very kind letter from a Lady-in-Waiting telling me Her Majesty was looking forward to reading the book and thanking me for my kind sentiments.

"Whether this played any part in the subsequent invitation to my wife and self to attend a garden party at Buckingham Palace I do not know, but it was a most enjoyable occasion, marred only by the distant sounds of sirens as ambulances and police cars raced towards the City to deal with a suspected terrorist attack. Friends' interpretation that the invitation was simply the first step on my way to the Tower proved entirely false – so far!"

Recalling his last year as chairman, Peter said the BBC in the New Year of 2005 introduced its *Voices* project to promote local accents and dialects and herald the end of the traditional 'Mummerzet' so beloved by radio and television producers when faced with the challenge of reproducing local speech and which FOND had been striving to eliminate since its inception in 1999.

"There are signs of some progress, wrote Peter, "with requests being received from producers for advice on our dialect, but there is still a long way to go.

"The BBC's project included setting up local discussion groups and it is rewarding to record that FOND's input, through the work of Tony Clarke, Jean Eaglen, Vera Youngman, Colin Burleigh and Bob Lister has been acknowledged in Simon Elmes's book, *Talking for Britain – A Journey Through the Nation's Dialects*."

As mentioned in Chapter 1, Tony Clarke produced and wrote the script for nine annual pantomimes at North Elmham Memorial Institute. Peter Brooks referring to the 2005 production, reported:

"Secretary Tony Clarke's reputation as a compiler of Norfolk dialect continued with his production of our annual pantomime, ably assisted by wife Pat in her role as wardrobe mistress. This time it was the unfortunate Peter Pan who underwent the Clarke treatment, assisted by members of FOND's executive committee and volunteers from the audience.

Tony Clarke's lavish production of Peter Pan at North Elmham Memorial Institute in January, 2005, when the cast included (left to right): Keith Skipper, John Nickalls, Peter Brooks, Audrey Foster, June Burleigh, and Glenda Burton.

"Again we had a capacity audience at North Elmham Memorial Institute and perhaps the essence of this annual extravaganza was summed up by one lady who echoed a similar comment a year earlier: 'So enjoyable, just what village entertainment was like before we had the box!' All proceeds from the pantomime, £453, were donated to the *EDP* 'Unicef Tsunami Disaster Appeal'."

Peter Brooks also reported that, in March, 2005, secretary Tony Clarke was invited to the National Maritime Museum to read a selection of original letters written by Lord Nelson to ascertain whether he wrote as he spoke, or vice-versa.

"Tony's conclusion was that Nelson certainly knew his native dialect, this being clear in sentence construction and phraseology. Nelson used no punctuation and only used capital letters for words he wished to emphasise."

Peter's final 12 months as chairman had begun at the AGM at the Lincoln Hall, Hingham, on November 21, 2004, when the speaker was the recently-retired Lord Lieutenant of Norfolk, Sir Timothy Colman, a FOND vice-president and contributor to *The Merry Mawkin's* 'What Norfolk Means to Me' series (Chapter 13).

Coincidentally, it was at the end of Peter's chairmanship and the beginning of Tony's that another distinguished 'What Norfolk Means to Me' contributor and FOND member was guest speaker at the 2005 AGM – Lord Walpole.

MEMORIES OF BRUTHER WILL

One of the regular entertainers during the first half of the North Elmham pantomime afternoons and at our Fond-dews was the late Bruther Will (aka William Johnson, of Middleton, near King's Lynn), always happy to fill in for a few minutes – or more – with his mouth organ recitals.

He was also a frequent correspondent to The Merry Mawkin, his address appearing as: Thuh Hovel, 1, Muckbarrer Farst, Littul Swearin', Near Cussen, Oathes.

CHAPTER 27

Editorial changes

Because of other commitments, after three years in the editorial chair of *The Merry Mawkin*, I stood down at the end of 2003, having given nine months' notice in the hope that a successor would be found in time to produce the spring edition in 2004.

However, when December 31 arrived, despite appeals in preceding *Mawkins* and at the October AGM, there had been no rush of applicants!

Chairman Peter Brooks was generous in his comments when he made his appeal at the AGM, saying that 'one of our outstanding successes has been the growth in size, content and appreciation of our quality newsletter, *The Merry Mawkin*.' He kindly claimed I had produced ten editions of what he considered to be 'one of the best, if not the best, magazine of its kind in the county'. Thank you, Peter.

It was Peter who, when the appeals for a new editor fell on deaf ears, commendably kept the newsletter in existence throughout 2004 and 2005 – compiling a total of eight editions – till I returned to produce the four editions of 2006.

The search continued in 2007 for a permanent editor, culminating in triumph with the appointment of **Ashley Gray** – author, graphic designer, artist and with a lifetime career in publishing and print design. Sighs of relief all round!

Before Ashley took over the *Mawkin* and produced a splendid new-style summer and autumn edition in 2007, there had been one more occupancy of the editorial chair when, in the spring, our technical officer, Stewart Orr, compiled Edition 25, in A4 format, neatly and efficiently covering the interregnum between my departure and Ashley's arrival.

Thus, *The Merry Mawkin* had survived a chequered history of editorial control which began, in tragic circumstances, just before Christmas 1999, as related in Chapter 2.

Peter Brooks wrote, in the combined summer and autumn edition of 2007, under the heading:

Welcome to our new editor

After a long period without an editor, your executive committee is delighted to announce the appointment of **Ashley Gray**, who lives in Wymondham, as the new editor and designer of *The Merry Mawkin*.

Ashley comes to us with a determination to build on the progress we have made to produce a lively and informative newsletter. He has lots of ideas and we are sure we shall be going from strength to strength under his guidance.

He will always be on the lookout for contributions and new contributors, and these are vital to ensure the newsletter is really 'yours' – and a means by which you can recall dialect words from the past you heard when you were young, or may have heard when you have been out shopping.

Ashley Gray: new editor of The Merry Mawkin and website co-ordinator.

Maybe you can remember certain dialect words used by your parents or grandparents, or perhaps you would just like to raise a question concerning our dialect or accent, or simply let's have your thoughts on what it means to live in Norfolk – good or bad!

Ashley joins us after a working life spent in print design at Jarrold Printing, once one of the leading printers in this country and all of Europe.

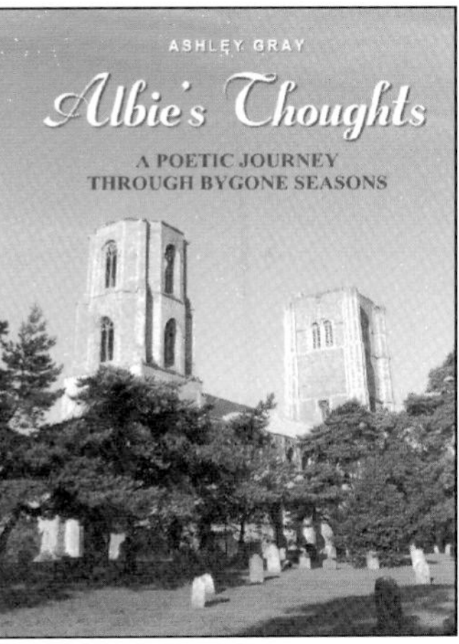

The two books of poetry by Ashley Gray, the new editor of The Merry Mawkin.

As well as being a graphic designer and artist, he is also the author of two books, both published in 2007: *Albie's Poems – Reflections of a Norfolk Lad*, an illustrated anthology of short poems, and *Albie's Thoughts – A Poetic Journey Through Bygone Seasons*.

In June, 2009, Ashley also became FOND's new website co-ordinator on the retirement of Pauline Dodd who, as reported in Chapter 10, had been in charge since FOND's website – www.norfolkdialect.com – had been set up in 2002, and, under her leadership, some 70,000 'hits' were recorded over the succeeding seven years.

FRIENDS OF NORFOLK DIALECT

The Merry Mawkin

£1

THE NEWSLETTER OF FRIENDS OF NORFOLK DIALECT

CONTENTS

The Chairman's Report	2	What the Harm a [illegible]?	10
Welcome to Our New Editor	2	Dora's Dumplins	10
From Our President	3	FOND Website	11
'Twixt Sea and Pine	4	Meet the Trunch Laureate	12
Notice of AGM 2007	5	We're Bin Orf Agin!	13
A Gem of an Aunt	6	Book Reviews	14
The Boy Colin's Norfolk Quiz	6	An Inflexible Friend	17
Blakeney Then and Now	7	Crossword Answers	18
'Dews' and Events	8	Norfolk Quiz Answers	19
From Our Young Mawkins	8	Something to Say?	19
Dialect Words Crossword	9	FOND Officers	20

website: http://www.norfolkdialect.com

The new-look Merry Mawkin, summer/autumn, 2007

CHAPTER 28

Fry Kingdom come!

AT THE END of June, 2006, Swaffham became the focus of some considerable media attention when it was announced that **Stephen Fry** was to appear in his first ITV drama for more than a decade – and the series would be set in a fictional Norfolk town.

Kingdom would star Fry as a country solicitor and Swaffham would take on the guise of Market Shipborough.

There was, of course, immediate speculation from members of FOND as to how the cast would cope with the Norfolk accent.

However, optimism arose when two members of FOND were asked to advise actors on the Norfolk dialect. They were life member Neil Storey and the man shortly to become chairman of FOND, Colin Burleigh, who, as a member of Equity, was also called on to take part in *Kingdom* as an 'extra'. Colin's experiences are related in the next chapter.

The *Eastern Daily Press* reported on June 30, 2006:

Stephen Fry set to return to our screens

One of Norfolk's most famous sons is poised to bring county life to the nation's screens in a new series.

In his first drama series for ITV since *Jeeves and Wooster* more than 10 years ago, Stephen Fry is set to star in a series set in a fictional Norfolk market town.

Kingdom stars Fry as Peter Kingdom, a country solicitor whose life is overshadowed by the mysterious death of his brother.

The six-part legal series is set in Market Shipborough, a

Stephen Fry: star of TV series Kingdom.

fictional Norfolk town, and centres on Kingdom's dysfunctional family. Hermione Norris and Celia Imrie also star in the series

Fry, who is also the executive producer, said: "*Kingdom* promises viewers a glimpse of the locations I love, and an hour in front of the television that will wash them in colours, textures, landscapes and characters that delight."

The series is being made in association with Fry's production company, Sprout.

Fry is intrinsically linked with Norfolk and recently became patron of the West Norfolk Literature group Centre Poets, taking over from former BBC Radio 4 presenter John Timpson, who died last year.

The comedian, actor and writer grew up at Booton, near Reepham, and briefly attended Gresham's School, Holt, before going to prep school in Gloucestershire.

He returned to Norfolk to resit his A-levels at the College of West Anglia and went on to study at Cambridge University.

As the filming of the new TV series *Kingdom* got under way at Swaffham, the *Eastern Daily Press* reported on July 14, 2006:

Dog turns to duck for Fry TV drama

BY NICKI WALKER AND VICKY LANGFORD

A quiet and unassuming Norfolk market town was a hive of activity yesterday as one of the county's most famous acting sons took to the streets to film his new TV series.

Stephen Fry, with an impressive cast, was in Swaffham to

Stephen Fry, Celia Imrie and Karl Davies filming in Swaffham...

record scenes for his first drama series for ten years. And the main focus of yesterday's filming was the Greyhound pub in Market Square which was picked as the local for the character played by Mr Fry, in the new series *Kingdom*.

The pub was given a slight makeover for the shooting, along with a name-change to The Startled Duck.

Landlord Nicky George, 37, said he didn't mind renaming his pub and was quite happy to hand over the bar for the day's shooting.

Mr George, who has been at the pub since 1972, said: "There's been a lot of interest from the locals and our regulars do not seem to mind that we have closed for the morning.

"I think it is good for the town of Swaffham. A few of the regulars have asked if we are going to keep the name The Startled Duck."

Landlady Joanne Briscoe added: "It's been really interesting to watch the filming and find out how it all comes together. Some of the scenes have been really funny."

Mr Fry said filming for the series would continue until October and the crew would be spending some time in Swaffham and other Norfolk locations.

...and Swaffham's Greyhound pub is reborn as The Startled Duck.

He said filming for the six-part legal series began on Monday and it was expected to be screened by ITV at the end of the year.

Among the cast members is Celia Imrie, star of *Dinner Ladies* and the film *Calendar Girls*.

Mr Fry, who lives in West Norfolk, said: "The people of Swaffham have been wonderful and very patient and we are going to be here for some months, so they will get used to seeing us around."

He said that in the series, Market Shipborough, unlike Swaffham, was near the sea. Nevertheless, he thought Swaffham was the ideal choice for the town, although filming would also take place at other venues in Norfolk.

Adrian Fitzpatrick, 33, from Swaffham said: "It's nice to see them filming here and it puts Swaffham on the map. I think it's funny that they have changed the name of the pub, and think they perhaps should keep it."

CHAPTER 29

Coaching Kingdom

ENCOURAGING NEWS for FOND came in the summer of 2006 when the producers of the Stephen Fry ITV series, *Kingdom*, based at Swaffham, contacted Norfolk historian and FOND life member **Neil Storey** to act as dialect adviser. And what's more, our **Colin Burleigh**, aka The Boy Colin, took part in the drama as an 'extra', and when Neil was unable to be present, helped coach the cast with their efforts to master the Norfolk accent.

Here is Colin's account of his experiences on and off the film set, from Edition 24 of *The Merry Mawkin*:

How film extra The Boy Colin also became dialect adviser to Stephen Fry actors

I reckon they're sin the Norfolk loight at larst!

When we cast our minds back to 1999, the year FOND was formed at Yaxham Village Hall, it will be recalled that apart from the fervent wish to preserve our beloved dialect we were 'up in arms' at the way our accent was never portrayed in the proper way by the TV and radio companies.

The actors inevitably spoke with voices that sounded as though they came from the West Country – to use Keith Skipper's word, from 'Mummerzet'. It has always been one of the major aims to try to make inroads into TV and radio to put this matter right.

Recently, I was called by my agent to take part as an 'extra' in the forthcoming Stephen Fry series, *Kingdom*, Nothing exciting there, you might say. However, my first two days on set involved watching a dyke-jumping competition as part of a crowd filmed at Barroway Drove, near Downham Market, and as a shopkeeper repairing a broken window.

What has this to do with FOND? you might ask. Well, I received another call from the agent who, aware that I am a member, asked if I would advise some of the cast on how to portray their characters with a Norfolk accent.

"They're sin the loight at larst!" I thought.

I was informed that their usual adviser, Neil Storey, FOND's life member, was unable to work on that day and I readily agreed to take his place.

After breakfast at base camp (June says I only go for the food!) I was introduced to actors Dan Ryan, Tony Slattery, Tom Fisher, Celia Imrie and Trevor Peacock and asked to go through the script with them to make suggestions as to how they should pronounce various words.

They were all keen to listen to what I had to tell them and, to be fair, some of them had done their homework and had obviously listened to what Neil had told them.

Tony Slattery, in particular, was keen to talk to me on the matter of the necessity to retain dialects and accents. Celia Imrie and her son Angus (also in the production) were a delight to work with and profuse in their thanks at the end of the shooting that day. I ate my lunch in the company of Trevor Peacock who was keen to discuss football (he supports Yeovil town) and cricket.

At the end of the day's filming I was asked to return the following day to go through the same procedure with other actors arriving on set, and I was keen to continue.

I successfully put the actors through their lines on the second day. The one thing that I noticed was that while I was rehearsing with them they could produce a reasonable accent, but when they got on the set in some cases their having to remember their lines tended to fog their memories for the accent. In many instances I had to step in and correct them. Still, I was enjoying the work and was pleased when I was asked to return for a third day.

At the end of the day I said my farewells, hoping our paths

might cross again some day — and they did, for I was called back again to do another day as an 'extra', this time, handing a plate of sandwiches to Rory Bremner!

The experience was a lot of fun, but underlying it all was the knowledge that maybe at long last the Norfolk accent may one day be portrayed on screen or over the airwaves in the manner that FOND would like it to be.

At least we've got a foot in the door. I look forward to seeing *Kingdom* on screen and will be listening avidly to hear if the effort Neil and I have put in has proved fruitful and trust that FOND can be proud of what has been done to try to knock 'Mummerzet' off our screens."

Neil Storey adds: It was a great pleasure to be part of the *Kingdom* project. Stephen Fry and all the cast and crew made it one of the most pleasurable jobs I have ever done. The set had a real 'family' atmosphere and I could tell everyone cared about the programme and showed a great respect for the cultural identity of our beloved county.

CHAPTER 30

More good news

AT ABOUT THE SAME TIME as *Kingdom* was being filmed at Swaffham, with the dialectal assistance of Neil Storey and Colin Burleigh, there was further encouragement for FOND during the summer of 2006 when the *Eastern Daily Press's* Cromer chief reporter Richard Batson revealed on August 11 that 'an international bevy of speech and drama teachers were heading to Norfolk for their summer git-tergether':

> TOUGH ONE: Keith Skipper's opportunity to show how real Norfolk is spuk
>
> ## Drama teachers join git-tergether for squit
>
> By Richard Batson
>
> Thass a rum'un. Them furriners keep tryin' ter larn tharselves Norfolk for when they go on the telly and stearge – but allus mearke a slummockin gret muddle onnit.
>
> Instead of sounding like good ole Norfolk bors and mawthers, they come out with a load of Mummerzet.
>
> So Sandringham-based soldiers in a poignant first world war drama sound more like the zider-swillin' Wurzels.
>
> But hope is on the horizon, as an international bevy of speech and drama teachers are heading to Norfolk for their summer git-tergether.
>
> They will be exposed to the local language, squit and a mardle on a Broads 'boot trip', as well as some 'wakkshops' at the

conference base, Gresham's School at Holt, more noted for the Queen's English than the Singing Postman's pronunciation.

Norfolk's missionary in residence is dialect champion Keith Skipper, who sees the event as a chance to stop further crimes against the county's spoken word. He is among the contributors to the four-day gathering of the Society of Teachers of Speech and Drama, running from August 17–20. Sixty delegates will watch plays, listen to folk songs, take part in puppet therapy and join in talks and lectures.

Mr Skipper sees it as a golden opportunity to show what real Norfolk sounds like – squit as she is spuk.

The Friends of Norfolk Dialect organisation, of which he was a founder, was formed in the wake of woeful accents in the BBC drama *All the King's Men.*

It was a tale of soldiers drawn mainly from the west Norfolk royal estate, who sounded as if they were 'members of the 1st Mummerzet Highlanders from a principality somewhere between Devon and Cornwall' said Mr Skipper.

Heydon, near Aylsham, where Weavers Green was filmed during the early 1960s.

Other dialect disasters included Anglia's 1960s soap *Weavers Green*, with Wendy Richard and Kate O'Mara, courtroom drama *Kavanagh QC*, starring John Thaw, and various productions of Arnold Wesker's Norfolk-set play, *Roots*.

Mr Skipper said actors were professional mimics whose job was to recreate accents, but he admitted Norfolk was a tough one to crack.

"It's partly the vocabulary, but also the vowels – which are impossible to write down and there are not enough of them. You have to listen to it."

Even before FOND was born he used to send tapes of spoken Norfolk to drama schools in the hope of righting the wrongs in the future.

"Norfolk has a specific dialect. There is not an all-purpose accent for East Anglia of a country bumpkin. It is hard to imitate.

"But you would not expect a play set in Birmingham to have Wolverhampton accents or a drama in Dublin to have Belfast voices.

"When I have complained in the past I have been told only we locals had noticed – but that ought to be enough."

He will be using excerpts from local literature such as The Boy John Letters and Colin Riches's Norfolk version of the Bible.

"I hope to get the message across with a lot of humour – and not be parsimonious or pompous. I am an enthusiast rather than an academic," Mr Skipper added.

CHAPTER 31

The Times takes notice

IN THE SUMMER EDITION of 2006, *The Merry Mawkin* reported that Norfolk schoolchildren were rediscovering the language of their forebears after the FOND education project, *Lost in Translation: An Exploration of the Norfolk Dialect*, was launched at a training day for teachers in March.

Chairman **Tony Clarke** reported: "Norfolk schoolchildren are recording the voices of dialect speakers, using equipment lent by FOND, and with the help of the Spin-off Theatre Company, learning new ways to interpret their cultural heritage through drama, art and dance.

"The recordings will eventually be lodged in the sound archive at the Norfolk Record Office, and the drama pieces should feature in exhibitions to be given at the Royal Norfolk Show, and later at The Forum, Norwich.

"FOND committee members are acting as links with their designated local schools, providing moral and practical support. The project, a partnership between FOND and the county council Children's Services Department, attracted wide media interest when we 'went public.'

"Coverage included interviews on national and regional TV, BBC Radio 4, BBC Radio Wales and stories in several national newspapers, including *The Economist*, the *Sun* and *The Times*, the latter giving us a page lead.

"The £24,600 project, funded through the Local Heritage Initiative, took a major step forward when the training day was held at the Norfolk Professional Development Centre on March 2. The programme included two lectures by FOND president, Professor Peter

Trudgill, dealing with accent, dialect, grammar and pronunciation.

"Spin-Off Theatre Company dealt with drama and music, and other speakers included Anna McCarthy, of the Children's Services Department – whose professional expertise is crucial to co-ordinating the project – FOND's technical adviser Stewart Orr (on the use of recording equipment), FOND's Peter Brooks and education officer Norman Hart, literacy advisers Emma Adcock and John Woodhouse."

And this was how *The Times* covered FOND's Norfolk schools project, as lead story on its Page 5 on March 23, 2006:

'He'yer fa' got a dickey, bor?' isn't rude... in Norfolk

It's a precious Fen dialect to be preserved in schools, writes ***Jonathan Richards***

When Norfolk schoolchildren are tussling in the playground the shout will no longer be: "That girl's teasing me!"

Instead, a victim might say: "I'm having a little bit of squit alonga the mawther." To add extra spite, the bully would be called 'slummican great mawther' – a fat young girl.

Tired of the misconceptions about the way people in Norfolk speak and concerned that their dialect – now spoken by only older members of the community – is slipping into oblivion, an action group called Friends of Norfolk Dialect (FOND) has successfully lobbied for schools to teach an appreciation of the local tongue.

The project, called *Lost in Translation*, which is supported by Norfolk County Council, has received £24,600 from the Local Heritage Initiative – an offshoot of National Heritage – and will be introduced in eleven schools from April.

"We've been waiting for this special day for a very long time," Norman Hart, vice-chairman of FOND, said. "I spent 30-plus years teaching in Norfolk schools and every dialect – West Indian, Scottish, Welsh – was to be welcomed, except one: Norfolk. That's just not good enough as far as we're concerned."

Keith Skipper, the Norfolk writer and broadcaster who co-founded FOND in 1999, said: "It's critically important that youngsters are aware that there's a wonderful, rich dialect that they need to use or lose. I wish there wasn't the need for this project, and that there was still a strong rhythm of proper language coming from the heart of the community. It's not something to be ashamed of."

Tim Groves, a teacher at Sheringham Primary, said most children would have had contact with the dialect only through their grandparents, but that with exposure, it was easy to understand.

The Times *feature was illustrated by a striking Broadland scene depicting 63-year-old Eric Edwards, described as 'one of the last of the Norfolk reedcutters', on board his boat piled high with neatly-cut bales. Also included on the page was this Norfolk dialect guide:*

GET BY IN NORFOLK

Do we go play on the titty totty tittermatorter?
Let's go and play on the very small see-saw.

That angle is slantendicular/on the huh.
That angle is not quite perpendicular/not straight.

I've got suffin goin about. I've got the uppards and downards.
I don't feel well. I've got diarrhoea.

I have a tizzick.
I have a troublesome cough.

He'yer fa' got a dickey, bor?
A Norfolk greeting, literally: Has your father got a donkey, boy?

The correct reply is...

Yis, an' he want a fule to roid him, will yew cum?
Meaning: Yes, and he wants a fool to ride him, will you come?

© *The Times, London, March 23, 2006*

Following the front page lead story on FOND's schools enterprise and *The Times* special feature, the *Mawkin* summer edition of 2006 also carried this encouraging report from our website co-ordinator, **Pauline Dodd**:

Instant reaction to our schools project

Already we've had a response on the website from one of the Norfolk children taking part in FOND's schools project. 'Eloise' made the following entry in our guestbook on May 18, 2006:

"We're doing a Norfolk dialect project at our school where we interview old Norfolk people. This site helped me with my homework. I can't wait till next Thursday when the Norfolk dialect people are coming in for the day."

In the next chapter we are given an eye-witness account of what happened on some of these school visits by, in Eloise's words, one of 'the Norfolk dialect people' – Colin Burleigh, aka The Boy Colin.

FOND technical adviser Stewart Orr recording some Norfolk words of wisdom from chairman Keith Skipper at the Tunstead Trosh in October, 2000. Also pictured (left to right) are Graham Kirk, Trosh organiser, Bill Bird and Barry Toyn.

CHAPTER 32

The Boy Colin goes back to school

LATER IN 2006, **Colin Burleigh** was to become FOND's fourth chairman, but earlier in the year he was one of the members who visited Norfolk schools to help spread the dialect gospel.

As already mentioned in Chapter 3, Colin has contributed a dialect article and a Norfolk quiz in every *Mawkin* since 2001. However, it was in the autumn edition of 2006 that for once The Boy Colin did not write in dialect, instead producing a moving account of his visits to Great Ryburgh and Stibbard primary schools, near Fakenham:

Was the FOND *Lost in Translation* project worthwhile? A thousand times, yes! declares The Boy Colin

The *Lost in Translation* project, which for many years was a dream for FOND and for Norman Hart, our education officer, in particular, finally dawned on us with the award of a Local Heritage grant, enabling us to make schools in the county aware of the rich heritage of our dialect.

I volunteered to be liaison officer for Great Ryburgh All Saints' Primary School, near Fakenham.

Having made contact with Claire Lawrence, the teacher involved, I was invited to attend the school on March 21. The children made me feel very welcome and the staff and teaching assistants were very helpful.

This would be my only visit to these premises, as the school was moving to a new site at Stibbard. On this visit I spoke to the children about accent and dialect words and found them keen and quick to learn.

Some told me how my accent and some of the dialect words were exactly as their grandparents spoke. I let them read poems by John Kett and put them right on the parts they could not pronounce.

It was on that visit that I learned that it was their intention to put on a play about the story of the Pedlar of Swaffham but it was their wish that it should be done in 'the Norfolk language'.

I volunteered to translate the script, written by Graham Hampton, another of the teachers involved, and following my submission of the original transmission, he visited me at home with more dialogue to which I gave my 'Norfolk' treatment. The script was then taken back to the school for the children to read.

On my next visit, this time to All Saints, Stibbard, they were rehearsing the play under the guidance of two members of the Spin-Off Theatre Group and while at the school I recorded all the characters on cassette to help get the accent correct. (Oh that the BBC and ITV would heed our advice on this matter!)

I received an invitation to see the production on June 16 and to give my opinion.

I was very pleased to hear how most of the main characters had mastered our native tongue and felt immensely proud of the children who had become very special to me. I was presented with a be-ribboned bottle of beer and a bouquet of flowers by the 'leading lady'.

I thought this would be the last occasion I would see the children, but I was invited to attend the Royal Norfolk Show with them and to hear them record the play for broadcasting on BBC Radio Norfolk's special programme on August 28, entitled *Fondly Speaking*, presented by Stewart Orr.

I also discovered that a DVD of the play had been produced and the children's parents had been snapping them up like hot cakes!

The day after the show I collected a woman reporter from *The Economist* at Norwich Station, taking her to Stibbard where she took notes as I put the children through their dialect vocabulary. I'm pleased to say they did me proud and had remembered most of the words I'd taught them.

They followed up with a run-through of the The Pedlar of Swaffham, the reading of some more John Kett poems and answered the reporter's questions intelligently. She was writing an article for *The Economist* on the project which has since been published.

Finally, my wife and I were invited to attend the children's end-of-term party where we were greeted with loud cheers and persuaded to join in the party games, together with eats and drinks.

A game of 'Pass the Parcel' was contrived to make me the winner – the prize being a blue All Saints fleece jacket, an idea thought up by the children.

Call me an old softy but it almost reduced me to tears. I have received an open invitation from the head teacher to go back to see the children whenever I wish to do so. I feel sure I shall see 'my children' again.

Was the *Lost in Translation* project worthwhile? From my point of view, a thousand times, yes. From the children's point of view, I sincerely believe it was.

CHAPTER 33

North to Louth!

AT THE END of his hard-hitting speech to the 2005 AGM (as recalled in Chapter 24), **Tony Clarke**, FOND's newly-elected chairman, declared: "Perhaps we can broaden our horizons by reaching out to dialect groups in other regions of England, trying to find out how they operate and exchanging ideas with them."

Only eight months later, Tony's dream was about to come true – not by FOND reaching out to a dialect group in another region of England, but by a dialect group in another region of England reaching out to FOND! And this was the front page lead story in the 2006 autumn edition of *The Merry Mawkin*:

Norfolk FOND attracts East Lincs links

By Robin Limmer

The fame of Friends of Norfolk Dialect, already reaching the ends of the earth through our website, has percolated, perhaps more unexpectedly, over our county's north-western border, culminating in an invitation for FOND members to visit the East Lincolnshire Dialect Society, known as Far-Welter'd*

As a result, a party of eight members of FOND are travelling to Louth on September 25 to meet their opposite numbers for an evening of discussion and entertainment.

**Far-Welter'd is a Lincolnshire term for an upturned sheep and is depicted in the society's logo.*

The initial approach was made by Far-Welter'd in July to our chairman, Tony Clarke, proposing closer contact with FOND and an invitation to visit them in Louth with a possible reciprocal visit by them to Norfolk.

Thus, after FOND's committee meeting in July, acting secretary Peter Brooks, closely involved with our schools project, contacted the Lincolnshire society and received an enthusiastic letter from their chairman, Alan Mumby, inviting FOND representatives to explain what was involved in achieving Far-Welter'd's long-term aims in creating a dialect archive available in a variety of media, from the written word through to DVDs.

FOND has already pioneered with Norfolk county educationists a project introducing an appreciation of the Norfolk dialect in schools and supplying recordings to the Norfolk Archive Centre at County Hall.

The Louth get-together will be reported on and discussed by our FOND committee on October 15.

In his letter to Peter Brooks, Far-Welter'd's Alan Mumby said the East Lincolnshire Dialect Society was formed in 1999 (by coincidence, the same year as FOND was inaugurated) and had a membership of 100, meeting about four times a year in pubs or village halls and entertaining with Lincolnshire dialect poems, tales and songs.

"We also send some of our dialect speakers out to events run by local organisations," wrote Mr Mumby. "Our long-term aim is to create a dialect archive available in a variety of media, from the written word through to DVDs. We'd also like to create an on-line, interactive platform. We'd like to think that this archive would be used by schools and the general public. You seem to have similar aims, although you appear to be a little further down the road than we are.

"It would be very useful for you to explain to our group what is involved in getting the funding to achieve our long-term aims – what work is involved and what the commitment is in general."

Mr Mumby suggested that a group of about six FOND members could be accommodated overnight in a local hotel or with families, adding: "And who knows what might develop out of that! Certainly, in the first instance, a return trip."

Commenting in the *Mawkin* on this development, Peter Brooks said: "The power of the Press has resulted in news of FOND's schools dialect project reaching all parts of the world, including East Lincolnshire!

"...Our committee has long believed that there is much to be gained by contacting and co-operating with similar-minded societies. Whatever our interests, be they dialect or deep-sea diving, nothing but good can come from an interchange of information and experiences."

And so, in the autumn, only a couple of months after Far-Welter'd's initial approach, an eight-strong FOND delegation headed north, led by chairman Tony Clarke, and it was Tony who later reported back to the *Mawkin's* winter edition of 2006 in his inimitable style:

When the mawkin met the upturned sheep

FOND FORGES THOSE EAST LINCS LINKS

by Tony Clarke

Have you heard what happened when the Fondites went to see the Far-Welter'ds? No? Well, for a price, we'll give you the full unexpurgated version.

For the moment, however, suffice it to say that two of the unsuspecting Fondites – who remain anonymous to protect the innocent – nearly got wrongly paired off when the overnight accommodation was being organised.

Everything got sorted out after they diplomatically explained that being members of FOND didn't mean they were *that* fond of each other!

From that auspicious opening onwards, laughter remained the dialect dish of the day when eight 'missionaries' from the Friends of Norfolk Dialect travelled to Louth in the beautiful Lincolnshire wolds to meet members of the East Lincolnshire Dialect Society, otherwise known as 'Far-Welter'd'.

It was probably to be expected that there would be a few comedians in any gathering of people from two organisations whose unconventional logos are a mawkin and an upturned sheep.

Upturned sheep: logo of the East Lincolnshire Dialect Society, Far-Welter'd.

Far-Welter'd, it seems, is a Lincolnshire term to describe a sheep which has been rolled on to its back and can't get up.

But there was a serious aspect to this exchange. Both FOND and Far-Welter'd are keen to make contact with other dialect societies to see how they all fit into the rich and colourful jigsaw of England's network of ancient regional languages.

The Lincolnshire folk were also keen to 'poach' information about FOND's successful education project among Norfolk schools in the hope that they can set up something similar.

During a Monday night session attended by about 80 enthusiasts in a village social centre at Great Carlton, near Louth, the two societies swapped stories, readings, jokes and song.

They also indulged in 'dialect tennis' in which they flung words and sayings at each other as a challenge to identify the meanings (pollywiggle – tadpole, was one Norfolk word which had 'em guessing!) The Norfolk visitors discovered they cannot claim exclusive ownership of the word 'squit'.

The FOND delegation – chairman Tony Clarke (aka The Boy Jimma) and his wife Pat, vice-chairman Norman Hart, Colin Burleigh (The Boy Colin) and his wife June, Ted Peachment, and John Austrin with his wife Liz (The Gal Liza) – enjoyed warm hospitality in Louth before returning to Norfolk the next day.

Said Tony: "It was a good exercise, which proved we in FOND, though we are proud of our Norfolk tongue, are not so parochial that we can't broaden our horizons and reach out to our neighbours.

"Our friendly little group was given the warmest of welcomes and I know our Lincolnshire friends would like to return the compliment by visiting Norfolk.

"Could this be the forerunner of future exchanges?"

Not many months later, in June, 2007, the compliment was indeed returned, when eleven members of Far-Welter'd visited Norfolk as guests of FOND and were entertained at a very well-supported evening of 'party-piece' variety at Swanton Morley Village Hall, arranged by FOND committee member Ted Peachment.

In September, 2008, our East Lincolnshire friends came back to Swanton Morley, and only a month later a FOND contingent of eight returned to Louth, as will be detailed in Chapter 41.

FOND stalwart and larger-than-life character **Mike Coley**, from Northwold in west Norfolk, a sufferer from multiple sclerosis, is dependent on his mobility scooter for getting around his home village, accompanied by his faithful Welsh terrier, Taffy (*pictured below*).

Together on July 25, 2006, they set off on a sponsored ride to visit nine churches, covering eighteen miles to raise money for the MS Trust.

Despite the vulnerability of a buggy on today's roads and the possibility that the battery might expire en route, Mike and Taffy triumphantly completed the expedition, calling at all nine churches – Didlington, Northwold, Methwold, Whittington, Stoke Ferry, Wretton, West Dereham, Boughton and Wereham.

And they raised £1,000 for the Multiple Sclerosis Trust at Letchworth Garden City, Hertfordshire.

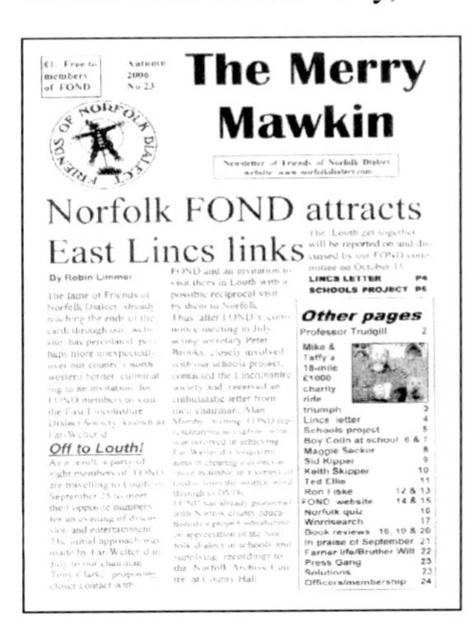

£1. Free to members of FOND

Autumn 2006 No 23

The Merry Mawkin

Newsletter of Friends of Norfolk Dialect
website: www.norfolkdialect.com

Norfolk FOND attracts East Lincs links

By Robin Limmer

The fame of Friends of Norfolk Dialect, already reaching the ends of the earth through our website, has percolated perhaps more unexpectedly over our county's north western border, culminating in an invitation for FOND members to visit the East Lincolnshire Dialect Society known as Far-Welter'd.

Off to Louth!

As a result, a party of eight members of FOND are travelling to Louth on September 25 to meet their opposite numbers for an evening of discussion and entertainment.

The initial approach was made by Far-Welter'd in July to our chairman Tony Clarke proposing closer contact with FOND and an invitation to visit them in Louth with a possible reciprocal visit by them to Norfolk.

Thus after FOND's committee meeting in July, acting secretary Peter Brooks, closely involved with our schools project, contacted the Lincolnshire society and received an enthusiastic letter from their chairman, Alan Mumby, inviting FOND representatives to explore what was involved in achieving Far-Welter'd's long-term aims in creating a dialect archive available in a variety of media from the written word through to DVDs.

FOND has already pioneered with Norfolk county educationists a project introducing an appreciation of the Norfolk dialect in schools and supplying recordings to the Norfolk Archive Centre at County Hall.

The Louth get-together will be reported on and discussed by our FOND committee on October 15.

LINCS LETTER P4
SCHOOLS PROJECT P5

Other pages

Professor Trudgill	2
Mike & Taffy's 18-mile £1000 charity ride triumph	3
Lincs letter	4
Schools project	5
Boy Colin at school	6 & 7
Maggie Secker	8
Sid Kipper	9
Keith Skipper	10
Ted Ellis	11
Ron Fiske	12 & 13
FOND website	14 & 15
Norfolk quiz	16
Wordsearch	17
Book reviews	18, 19 & 20
In praise of September	21
Farmer life/Bruther Will	22
Press Gang	23
Solutions	23
Officers/membership	24

CHAPTER 34

A Norfolk partnership

MEANWHILE, there was a general sense of satisfaction and achievement at the increasing success of the schools project partnership between FOND and the education department of Norfolk County Council. Pictures and report in the *Mawkin's* autumn edition, 2006:

FOND and schools' pioneering initiative deemed great success

By Peter Brooks, acting secretary

The partnership between FOND and Children's Services of Norfolk County Council to introduce an appreciation of our local dialect into schools across the county has been a great success.

All the right signs had been there for this groundbreaking initiative – enthusiastic teachers and children who had enjoyed taking part in the project, some wonderful material in the recordings made by pupils and teachers, and the creation of links between the schools and their local communities.

For example, Brancaster Primary pupils went into the community to talk to elderly people in residential homes.

A bonus was the media interest, local and national, with pupils, teachers and FOND members in radio, Press and television interviews. Our technical officer, Stewart Orr, sourced all the recording equipment, ensuring everyone knew how to use it, collating some 200 recordings and produced an hour-long programme for BBC Radio Norfolk.

The culmination of the project was a week-long display of the schools' work at the Forum in Norwich. Visitors could hear the dialect recordings made by the Brancaster pupils, read the dialect dictionary compiled by pupils at Langham School and watch videos, such as a play based on the Pedlar of Swaffham, by All Saints' Primary School, Great Ryburgh, and a song and dance performance by pupils at Sheringham Primary.

There were stories from Diss High School and Firside Middle, Norwich, who also provided a range of Norfolk puppets.

Congratulations to FOND vice-chairman and education officer, Norman Hart, kingpin of the project. Thanks also to Anna McCarthy, arts development officer, Children's Services, and Gill Seaton, of arts development administrative assistance.

The project was funded by the Local Heritage Initiative, a partnership between the Countryside Agency, Heritage Lottery Fund and the Nationwide Building Society, whose William Wall, Eastern region adviser, gave invaluable support.

Praise, too, for the Spin-Off Theatre Company's dialect performances and traditional Norfolk music. The future? A report on the project, examining its highs and lows and bringing together all who took part to discuss the lessons learned in raising the profile of our county dialect.

We're encouraged by a Norfolk head mistress who said she plans to include work on Norfolk dialect in her school's curriculum next year, and by a Scottish head who said she would strive to include Scottish dialect in a similar project to FOND's.

Lost in Translation recordings take their place in our archives

Stewart Orr, FOND technical adviser, wrote in the winter *Mawkin*, 2006: A major part of the FOND *Lost in Translation* project was the collection of a large number of recordings to be made by schools and returned to us at FOND.

You may even have heard of some of them, either at the Forum, Norwich, or in the programme *Fondly Norfol*k on BBC Radio Norfolk on August Bank Holiday Monday.

FOND president Professor Peter Trudgill is interviewed by EDP reporter Caroline Culot, recorded by our technical adviser, Stewart Orr, at the week-long display of schools' work at the Forum in Norwich in July, 2006.

Yes, they have started to come in, and superb many of them are, too. They range from the very brief, lasting a minute or two, to the unstoppable characters who "go on" (gloriously) for almost an hour.

Also the sound quality is generally very good, so these new recordings sit well alongside those recorded by the FOND stalwarts over the last few years and already in our archives.

Of the nine schools involved we asked for 20 recordings from each, totalling 180. As we have 84 recordings returned, we are a little under half way there.

It was a delight to produce *Fondly Norfolk*, a feature programme about the project, for Radio Norfolk. In the past I have worked hard to make original recordings for similar August Bank Holiday features, but this time I would think a good 20 minutes' material came straight from the schools recordings themselves – a great testimony to the quality of their work.

Copies of their original recordings are being returned on CD to the schools concerned. Eventually copies will be available to members and others from FOND's own archives, and there will also be listening copies lodged with Jonathan Draper at the Norfolk Record Office.

CHAPTER 35

Colin, fourth chairman

AFTER ITS HIGHEST PROFILE twelve months so far, FOND, founded in 1999, has launched into a new year full of optimism and new ideas designed to build on past success – and with a new man at the helm.

That was the opening paragraph in the lead story in the *Mawkin's* 24th edition, reporting on the AGM held at the Lincoln Hall, Hingham, on November 26, 2006.

Colin Burleigh (aka The Toff of Toftwood and The Boy Colin) was elected chairman in succession to Tony Clarke (The Boy Jimma), FOND's secretary for six years and chairman for one.

Colin Burleigh: FOND's fourth chairman.

Tony said he was standing down for personal reasons (*only a few of us knew it was because of his terminal ill-health, as explained in Chapter 1*).

John Austrin was among those who paid warm tribute to Tony's services as secretary and chairman.

Colin, a committee member since FOND's inception, thus became the organisation's fourth chairman, after Keith Skipper, Peter Brooks and Tony.

Born at Dereham in 1931, Colin attended Hamond's Grammar School, Swaffham. He worked for Jentique Furniture before RAF National Service and when stationed in Germany would regale his colleagues with 'News from Dumpton' in the *Dereham and Fakenham Times*.

On demob he joined the Collegians Jazz Band as singer, remaining with them for 36 years. After redundancy at Jentique he sold menswear till redundancy struck again, then joined Jarrolds as a furniture salesman. After the demise of the Collegians he joined the Vintage Hot Orchestra as drummer/vocalist, and to date has been with them 21 years.

Colin appeared regularly on BBC Radio Norfolk in Keith Skipper's *Dinnertime Show* and later with the Press Gang.

"With a bit of jazz, a touch of comedy and a happy home life with June, and being blessed with children and grandchildren, I think I can say I'm a contented man," he reflected.

Keith, writing in the *Mawkin* about FOND's new leader, said: "The Toff of Toftwood is ready for high office. Colin Burleigh's sartorial elegance, comic élan and musical prowess make him a complete performer on the local entertainment circuit

"Now the catwalk of culture beckons as he dons the robes of linguistic loquacity to become the fourth chairman of Friends of Norfolk Dialect – a role simply waiting for his towering talents.

"I dubbed him 'The Toff of Toftwood' when he turned those quickfire quips of various vintages into a stage routine so reminiscent of the old vaudeville pedlars of mirth. His snazzy shirt and waistcoat set him apart from the rest."

Keith added: "Colin has insisted many times that humour is the shock-absorber of life. It helps us take the blows. He is living proof of such a creed, returning to the entertainment fray with even more zest after taking his scripts to 'Happy Pappy' (Papworth Hospital) and adding memorable lines about having 'four bypasses in ten hours… and that's more than the whole of Norfolk has had in twenty years'."

Colin Burleigh's first **Boy Colin** article appeared in Edition 3 of *The Merry Mawkin* in the spring of 2001 and the series has continued in every edition since. Colin's 'Norfolk Quiz' has also been a regular feature, the first one gracing the *Mawkin* pages in Edition 4, autumn, 2001.

The Boy Colin sagas were normally written in broad Norfolk, but two exceptions have already appeared in this book. In Chapter 29 Colin wrote in conventional style an account of his experiences as a dialect adviser and film extra on the set of the TV series *Kingdom*, and in Chapter 32, 'The Boy Colin Goes Back to School', he told how he was one of the FOND members who visited Norfolk schools to help spread the dialect gospel.

Over the years, The Boy Colin series recounted schooldays at Dereham and Swaffham, National Service in the RAF in the UK and Germany, jazz band nights, Carrow Road, holidays at home and abroad and comprehensive recollections of life in his beloved county. Here's an example: the very first Boy Colin contribution to the *Mawkin* in the spring of 2001:

LOOKIN' BACKARDS

Cod liver oil an' malt kep' us a'gorn

When yer gotta bit o' spare time, an' blarst I're had plenty o' that leartly, ent that a rummin how yew allus think about when yew wuz a kid? People orfen say they were the best times, but wuz they?

My parents never had much, ony kids, but at least they kep' a eye on us an' knew what we wuz up to. Not like nowadays when kids are left to run riot orl over the plearce, a'kickin' up a shine.

We et well, thow kids terday would tarn thare snouts up at some o' the things we had. Mother use ter mearke a suet pudden nearly evra day an' we'd hev half onnit with meat an' grearvy, an' fer arters we'd hev the rest onnit with a spoonful o' triggle.

Granfer kep' a' farm, tho that wuz sposed ter keep him, an' we were lucky enow ter hev the occasional ow rabbit. I asked Father how Mother kep' the crust up on har rabbit pies and he reckon she used humpty-back rabbits. I never did know whether he wuz a'tellin' on the truth.

FOND'S own cheeky chappie, Colin Burleigh, drummer and vocalist with the Vintage Hot Orchestra for the past twenty-one years.

DING O' THE LUG

We never had real pork sossages, they tearsted like bread crumbs. Father reckon thas cause they coon't mearke both ends meat! If we din't hev much, we had a few laughs, thow I allus got a ding o' the lug gollopin' my grub into me so fast.

Come autumn the hull family went out blackburra pickin'. We use to clawk them ow brumbles down with a croom an' fill our ow barskets wi' grit ow blackburras, then tearke 'em orf to the shop where Frank Edwards use ter weigh 'em and pay us for 'em. I allus wondered why a bloke what kep' a radio shop wanted blackburras fer, but the money allus paid for our winter coats, least so Mother say.

SUNDAY SKULE

The bloke what lodged longa Aggie Legood, down our yard, worked fer Eldorado Ice Cream Company and peddled a trike wi a box on the front. Hot summer days (yis, we use ter get 'em then) Mother use ter get us a thrippenny ice cream orf him fer a treat, an' slice it in ter three bits on a sorcer. That wuz livin', I'll tell yer.

Time we were four year old we went to Sunday skule at St Withburga's which wuz ony about 50 yard from where we lived. Old Polly Oliver took us fer lessons an' she used to comter Sunday skule a'pushin' a grit ow sit-up-an-beg bike wot han't got no pedals onnit.

That turned out she never could ride a bike but she liked it fer a support an' had the pedals took orf so they din't keep a'knockin' aginst har shins.

Friday night wuz bath night an' we had an ow tin bath in front o' the fire plearce. The water cum in from the wash-house acrorss the yard where that had bin heated in the ow copper.

My sisters got dun farst an' I hatta bath in the searme water arter them. I allus hoped there wunt too much sludge in the bottom. I din't like winter time bathing cors I wuz allus afreard the logs on the fire would crackle and I'd get bant by the sparks.

GOOD OW SPUNFUL

Still a bath once a week and a good ow spunful o' cod liver oil an' malt kep' us a'gorn. That musta stood us in good stead corse we're still here to tell the tearle.

I could run on for hours 'bout them days, but I better finish now. I kin remember lots o' things from way back, but arsk me if it wuz rearnin' last Friday, or what I had fer dinner on Monday an' I coon't tell yer. Thas a failin' we all hev when we get old, ent it?

The ony blessin' 'bout gettin' old is that yew kin hide yer own Christmas presents!

CHAPTER 36

Keith Skipper MBE DL

FOND'S FOUNDER-CHAIRMAN **Keith Skipper**, already a Deputy Lieutenant of Norfolk, was made a Member of the Order of the British Empire in the New Year Honours for 2007.

The 2007 New Year Honours List was published in advance on Saturday, December 30, 2006, and the *Eastern Daily Press* led the page of East Anglian recipients with the banner headline:

Keith Skipper, MBE, after the award ceremony at Buckingham Palace.

Norfolk's mardling MBE

By Richard Batson

His elevation to an MBE is, to use the dialect Keith Skipper cherishes and champions, 'a rum owd dew'.

The writer, entertainer and broadcaster is celebrating getting a New Year honour for service to the community in his beloved Norfolk... including helping to raise charity cash through his Press Gang shows and founding a dialect 'supporters' club'.

But Mr Skipper said it was ironic that his 'proud

parochialism', which saw him sacked from BBC Radio Norfolk in 1995 for bemoaning the lack of localness in the programming, had now won him an honour. Toying with his new-found 'nobility', he reckoned it stood for 'My Bewtiful Embellishment' – and mockingly mumbled he would rather have been a CBE as it stood for Chronicler, Broadcaster and Entertainer.

Mr Skipper, 62, was born at Beeston, near Dereham, and went to Hamond's Grammar School, Swaffham, before embarking on a 17-year stint with the *Eastern Daily Press* at Thetford, Dereham, Yarmouth and Norwich.

After a 'gap year' of cricket and strawberry picking in 1979, he joined Radio Norfolk at its inception, until the parting of the ways in November, 1995 – which allowed him to tackle the wider range of activities which has led to his award.

"It provided the incentive and the time to do things there would not have been time for if I had been in full-time employment," he explained.

That saw him leading the Press Gang, now in their 24th season, around hundreds of village halls, raising thousands of pounds for local causes, including rattling buckets for the *EDP's* own 'We Care' appeal.

He also organised a series of Aristosquits concerts at Wolterton Hall, where the county's great and good did party pieces, again raising funds for 'We Care'.

When he became one of the great and the good himself three years ago, having become a Deputy Lieutenant, he persuaded his other 'DLs' to do a turn for the same cause.

But Mr Skipper is best known for his love of the Norfolk dialect and was founder-chairman of the Friends of Norfolk Dialect, set up in 1999 to 'promote and preserve' the local tongue, especially in the face of a spread of 'Mummerzet' accents in film, TV and radio dramas. Their work has now moved into schools to encourage youngsters to take a pride in their dialect.

He has also released many books, CDs and videos about Norfolk and is a popular after-dinner speaker.

Reflecting on his MBE, he said: "I have been writing and mardling about Norfolk and its unique character for a living and

Keith Skipper's Larn Yarself Norfolk was reprinted by permission of Terry Davy's widow, Shirley, and is still a best seller.

for pleasure since 1962 – and remain constantly inspired by a county of which I never tire."

The next challenge was to ask his old marshman friend Eric Edwards, MBE, how a country boy should dress to meet the Queen, who was sent a copy of Mr Skipper's *Larn Yarself Norfolk* book after it was revealed she did dialect impressions as a family after-dinner entertainment.

"If she tells me I look like a mawkin, I will know I have failed the fashion test, but that she has read the book," he chuckled.

MBE? It stands for My Bewtiful Embellishment, says Skip.

The writer, entertainer and broadcaster received his award for service to the community in his beloved Norfolk... Including helping to raise thousands of pounds of charity cash through his Press Gang shows and co-founding Friends of Norfolk Dialect.

CHAPTER 37

Kingdom – dismay at second coming

A FEW MONTHS after the screening of *Kingdom*, the TV drama series set in the fictional Norfolk town of Market Shipborough, starring Stephen Fry, came reports of a sequel.

On August 22, 2007, this was how, in his **Skipper's Log** column in the *Eastern Daily Press*, Keith greeted the news:

Out of Fry's panned series – and into the ire

The second coming of *Kingdom* seems destined to provoke an angry repeat chorus of complaints.

My media spies tell me the follow-up series of ITV's show starring Stephen Fry and dear old Swaffham betrays no extra efforts to capture the authentic Norfolk sound.

Indeed, there are strong rumours that dialect experts called in to advise cast and producers before last April's launch have been shunned altogether this time.

Despite constant reminders about boosts for our local economy, especially when it comes to tourism, those of us who have complained about Mummerzet tones in national television and radio productions since time immoral are ready for yet another crusade.

Stephen Fry can hardly be surprised we've got our danders up. He is happy to flash his 'made in Norfolk' badge when it suits him and he must be aware of protests rumbling on since so many of his *Kingdom* colleagues got the accent hideously wrong.

His Norfolk roots ought to have turned red with embarrassment as letters and articles in the *EDP* highlighted so much bitter disappointment with the first six instalments. 'Dubbing is the only answer', read one curt verdict.

Keith Skipper continued:

While Mr Fry remains silent on the matter, an international expert in the dialect field is unfurling the Norfolk flag with timely vigour. **Professor Peter Trudgill** truly relishes his local connections.

Pointing strongly to the *Kingdom* kerfuffle, he launches his series on 'How Not to Make Norfolk People Cross' in the latest edition of *The Merry Mawkin*, Friends of Norfolk Dialect's newsletter.

The professor, born in Norwich, with all his 16 great-great-grand-parents coming from the east of the county, has been FOND president since the oganisation was set up in 1999.

His educational check-list to be consulted before every rehearsal and every take is aimed at actors trying to reproduce the proper accent in any forthcoming Norfolk-based drama.

Basic level deals with how not to sound as if you come from somewhere else. Introductory level shows how to start sounding just a little bit like you do come from Norfolk.

Keith added:

In the next edition, Professor Trudgill will move on with help on how to sound even more like you come from Norfolk with an exciting and special section on the Norfolk long 'o'.

Perhaps he feels the current *Kingdom* crew are beyond redemption, but it would do them a power of good to invite FOND's president for an enlightening mardle. After all, there could yet be a third series centred on the fleshpots of Swaffham.

In the longer term, those who persist in setting a drama in Norfolk without respecting native sounds and sensibilities will find it even harder to escape censure.

They must ignore the braying of 'celebrity blow-ins' who reckon they've just about done the county if they take the doggy for a canter on Holkham beach!

Professor Peter Trudgill: spurred on by the return of TV's Kingdom, with its Mummerzet accents, the Norfolk-born dialect expert has taken up the challenge of teaching outsiders how to sound as if they come from around here.

FRY FRIPPERY

Following Keith Skipper's comments that Stephen Fry is happy to flash his 'made in Norfolk' badge when it suits him, Nancy Wedge interviewed Fry for the *Eastern Daily Press Norfolk Magazine* in February, 2009, and expressed surprise that a chat was granted.

For eight months earlier, this was what she was told by his sister and personal assistant, Jo Crocker: "Stephen rarely gives full-blown interviews these days and very politely declines your request."

Nancy Wedge wrote: "Like the rest of the Fry family, Jo is based in Norfolk and has been her brother's personal assistant since he was the bit-part star of Cambridge Footlights at university.

"So on discovering that the private Mr Fry was coming to Norwich department store Jarrold to sign copies of his latest book, *Stephen Fry in America*, it came as a surprise that a chat was granted."

When she asked him about his reluctance to give interviews, he responded: "I am only doing it for you as you are Norfolk. I did them so much when I was starting out; I prefer not to do them these days."

FOND FLOUTED

I had experienced Stephen Fry's propensity to distance himself from journalists when, as editor of *The Merry Mawkin*, I wrote to him in January, 2003, asking if, with his close association with Norfolk, he would write a piece for the newsletter.

Stephen Fry enjoying a game at Carrow Road.

However, on Stephen Fry notepaper, I received an apologetic letter from sister Jo Crocker stating: "Sadly, as I had rather expected, he cannot find the time to write an article for either the summer or autumn edition because of the huge amount of time he must dedicate to post-production on *Bright Young Things*, which is due for release at the end of this year."

Undaunted, eight months later, I wrote again to Mr Fry, this time to his Norfolk home, to ask if perhaps he might be able to write something for the winter edition of the *Mawkin*.

It was Jo Crocker who replied from London: "Stephen is dreadfully sorry that he is not able to grant your request because he is about to enter possibly the busiest three months of his career. After the UK opening of the feature film he has directed, *Bright Young Things*, Stephen leaves for Australia, New Zealand and America which takes him to mid-December. Sadly there won't be a moment for writing. With many apologies again and best wishes for the future, Yours sincerely, Jo Crocker."

Oh well, I tried (twice)!

CHAPTER 38
Sid Kipper

COMEDIAN SID KIPPER has contributed to the columns of every *Merry Mawkin* since Edition 2 in the summer of 2000, just ahead of Colin Burleigh's Boy Colin episodes which began their marathon editorial run some six months later in the spring of 2001.

In Chapter 2 we mentioned that Keith Skipper had said of Sid that 'the self-styled megastar combines writing, singing and story-telling in such seamless fashion it is difficult to know where to fit him on the entertainment menu'.

And it was Keith who, in his book, *Confessions of a Norfolk Squit Merchant*, published in 2008 by Halsgrove, wrote: "A modest megastar from the parish of St Just-near-Trunch merged as Norfolk's leading cultural ambassador of recent times – by breaking most of the rules.

"Sid Kipper defied tradition by taking on missionary work beyond home shores. That meant he was cast for too long as a prophet without real honour on his own midden. He refused to compromise, however, and his potent mixture of squit and culture eventually collected deserved plaudits...

Sid Kipper: modest megastar.

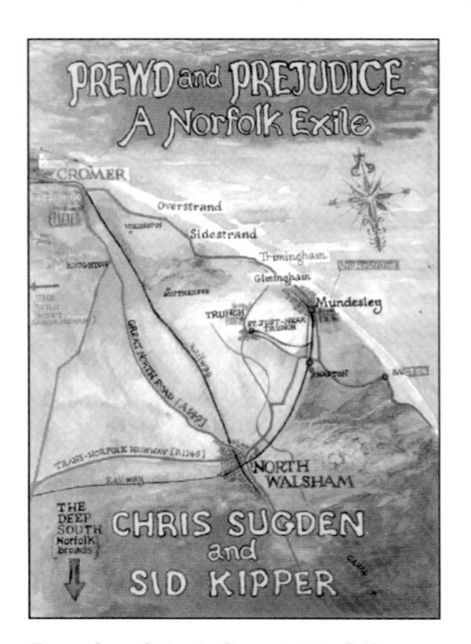

Prewd and Prejudice, A Norfolk Exile, by Chris Sugden and Sid Kipper, published by Mousehold Press.

"Perhaps 'talented all-rounder with sideways stance' offers the most useful clue to the skills of a performer behind such classics as *Prewd and Prejudice*, *The Crab Wars*, *David Kipperfield*, *The Pied Blowpiper of King's Lynn*, *Three Gruff Billy Goats*, *Bunfight at the OK Chorale (set in the old Tame East)* and the local vicar's *Letters to the Truncheons*. Now what would the Boy John make of those?

"Sid takes his distinctive brand of humour all over the country and occasionally abroad to show Norfolk is way ahead of the field when it comes to lateral thinking.

"Happily, his constant homecomings now attract full rations of adoration."

For a good example of Sid's contributions to *The Merry Mawkin* we go back to that very first article published in Edition 2 in 2000:

Talking Norfolk

A few words from FOND member Sid Kipper

I get to go all around the country in my line of work and talking Norfolk can get you in a proper old muddle in foreign parts.

For an instance, I done this here interview in Yorkshire, where this bloke asked me about a particular concert what I'd done. So I told him how before the concert there was a queue outside. Well, he looked at me gone out.

He say did I mean there was an armed uprising? So I say No, what was he on about? And he say never mind that, what was I on about talking about a queue outside?

Well, we din't get it straight until I told him what a queue was. Then he say, "Oh, you mean a kew," so I say No – tha's a place in London where they grow erotic plants.

Then there's bowls. You talk about a bowls match in Devon or Dorset and any of them Shires and they think you're talking dirty.

My old Uncle George has writ a song what helps explain some of this:

When we have a do then the grass is all wet,
A thud's one divided by three.
We stand in a coup when we've something to get.
And hare's where we happen to be.
'Cos we're Norfolk Dumplings, we do different too;
Abroad's what we sail on, but what's that to you?

Anyoldhow, I shall carry on talking proper, you can rest assured. Because like my old mother Dot always say, when the going gets rum, the rum get going. She always say that. I wonder what it mean?

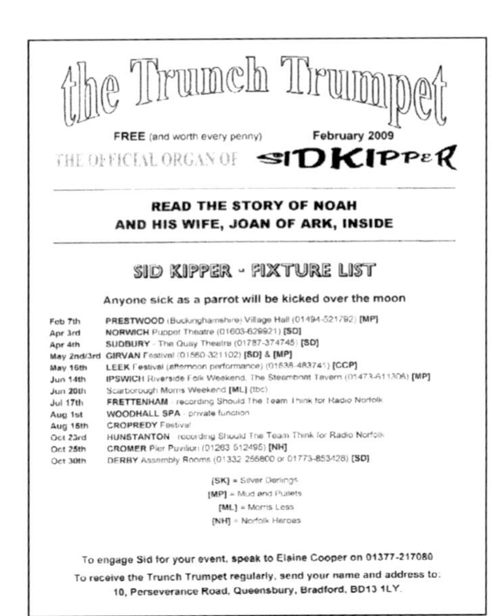

the Trunch Trumpet

FREE (and worth every penny) February 2009

THE OFFICIAL ORGAN OF SID KIPPER

READ THE STORY OF NOAH AND HIS WIFE, JOAN OF ARK, INSIDE

SID KIPPER - FIXTURE LIST

Anyone sick as a parrot will be kicked over the moon

Feb 7th	PRESTWOOD (Buckinghamshire) Village Hall (01494-521792) [MP]
Apr 3rd	NORWICH Puppet Theatre (01603-629921) [SD]
Apr 4th	SUDBURY - The Quay Theatre (01787-374745) [SD]
May 2nd/3rd	GIRVAN Festival (01560-321102) [SD] & [MP]
May 16th	LEEK Festival (afternoon performance) (01538-483741) [CCP]
Jun 14th	IPSWICH Riverside Folk Weekend, The Steamboat Tavern (01473-611306) [MP]
Jun 20th	Scarborough Morris Weekend [ML] (tbc)
Jul 17th	FRETTENHAM - recording Should The Team Think for Radio Norfolk
Aug 1st	WOODHALL SPA - private function
Aug 15th	CROPREDY Festival
Oct 23rd	HUNSTANTON - recording Should The Team Think for Radio Norfolk
Oct 25th	CROMER Pier Pavilion (01263 512495) [NH]
Oct 30th	DERBY Assembly Rooms (01332 255800 or 01773-853428) [SD]

[SK] = Silver Derings
[MP] = Mud and Pullets
[ML] = Morris Less
[NH] = Norfolk Heroes

To engage Sid for your event, speak to Elaine Cooper on 01377-217080

To receive the Trunch Trumpet regularly, send your name and address to: 10, Perseverance Road, Queensbury, Bradford, BD13 1LY.

The Trunch Trumpet – 'The Official Organ of Sid Kipper.'

Sid's regular newsletter contains not only his 'fixture list' of the venues he'll be appearing at all over the country (from Cornwall to Scotland) but also some of his stories, including, for instance, 'Noah and his wife, Joan of Ark'.

Also listed are details of his books, CDs and cassettes.

The Trunch Trumpet, says Sid, is 'free (and worth every penny).'

CHAPTER 39

More national publicity

WITH *The Merry Mawkin's* new editor Ashley Gray now comfortably settled into the editor's chair, chairman **Colin Burleigh** reported in the 2007 winter edition how FOND had attracted more national publicity during a BBC Radio 4 broadcast:

"We achieved a bit more national coverage on October 5th when I was asked to talk on the BBC Radio 4 lunchtime programme *You and Yours* with presenter John Waite.

"Taking part were the Appledorians (a Devon dialect association with similar aims to FOND), Professor Peter Patrick of Essex University and myself.

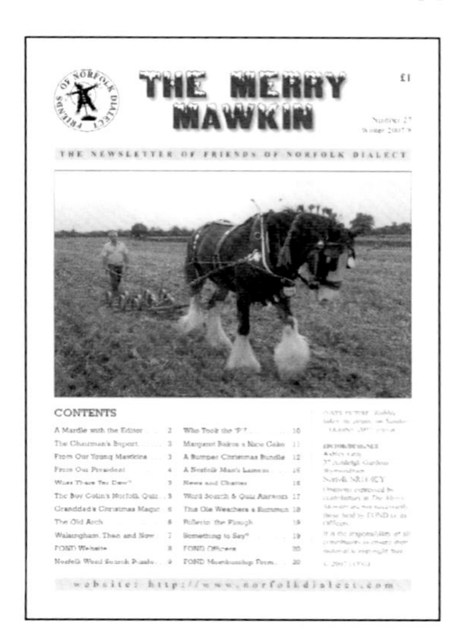
FRIENDS OF NORFOLK DIALECT

THE MERRY MAWKIN

£1

THE NEWSLETTER OF FRIENDS OF NORFOLK DIALECT

CONTENTS

A Mardle with the Editor 2
The Chairman's Report 3
From Our Young Mawkins 3
From Our President 4
The Old Arch 6
Walsingham Then and Now 7
FOND Website 8
A Bumper Christmas Bundle 12
News and Chatter 16
Word Search & Quiz Answers 17
FOND Officers 20
FOND Membership Form 20

website: http://www.norfolkdialect.com

Settled in the editor's chair: Ashley Gray's Merry Mawkin, winter 2007.

"None of the speakers really had much time to put their points of view on dialect across, but I did get the chance to tell of our schools project and to slip in a few choice Norfolk words and phrases.

"In the short time allowed I was able to make people aware of our aims and I gather it was well received."

Incidentally, in 2006 Colin had been invited by BBC Television to take part in the children's show *Dick and Dom in da Bungalow* to demonstrate the Norfolk dialect to an audience of millions. His wife June acted as translator!

After describing how the invitation came about, including an interview on BBC Radio Norfolk explaining what was going to happen on the television show, Colin wrote in the *Mawkin's* summer edition of 2006:

> On our arrival at Liverpool Street, a mobile phone message guided us to a swish red Rover with my name on a placard in the window and June and I were whisked like royalty across to North Acton where hotel accommodation had been arranged.

After an evening theatre visit to see *The Lion King* and breakfast the next morning , a taxi took Colin and June to BBC Television Centre in Wood Lane...

> We were ushered into a room to meet other folk appearing on the show, before being taken to 'make-up'.
>
> We were complimented on our complexion by the make-up girls who decreed that we didn't require their services – it says something for our fresh air in Norfolk.
>
> We were then 'miked-up' and waited to be shown to the studio. On inquiring if a rehearsal would take place, we were told it would prove funnier without!
>
> Dick and Dom, together with Sarah Cox, a BBC Radio 1 DJ, and the children awaited us in the studio and we sailed straight into the routine.
>
> Everyone was amused and mystified by the phrases I trotted out, and June played her part excellently as translator. It was over all too quickly and we left the studio for yet another taxi to take us back to Liverpool Street. Before we left, I had the chance for a short chat with football pundit Graeme le Saux.
>
> We caught our train back to Norwich at the end of what had been a hilarious but nevertheless worthwhile experience.

Colin's experiences with radio and TV were possibly a sequel to a BBC nationwide *Voices* project the previous year, pledging to cherish regional dialects. A full-page feature in the *Eastern Daily Press* of January 17, 2005, proclaimed:

BBC vows to portray
the true voice of Norfolk

After explaining how the formation of FOND came about, *EDP* reporter Ian Clarke wrote:

> FOND has gone from strength to strength in promoting the Norfolk accent and hopes the BBC's *Voices* project will help in its efforts.
>
> The initiative has several strands including audio gatherers recording the voices of at least 1,000 interviewees from a mix of people across the country. People will also be able to have their say about accents, and linguistic academics are involved to create an online interactive dialect map.
>
> Mick Ord, project director for the *Voices* project, said: "We're combining BBC journalism and storytelling with academic input and rigour to bring to life in an accessible and entertaining way a linguistic blueprint for Britain."
>
> To mark the launch of the project, the BBC is publishing results of a major survey of 5,000 people on accents.
>
> It reveals that people love accents such as those of silver-tongued Scottish actor Sean Connery, newscaster Trevor McDonald and veteran radio presenter Terry Wogan.
>
> But the likes of Irish politician Ian Paisley, TV personality Janet Street-Porter and Scottish comedian Billy Connolly are most likely to have people reaching for the 'off' switch.
>
> The survey also reveals how proud we are about accents and what it does for prestige and increasing chances of succeeding at a career.
>
> Dr Clive Upton, a linguistics expert at Leeds University, said: "Scratch the surface and language can create huge debate. We are passionate about it because it's about our identity, who we are and where we are from."

The *EDP* feature included a large colour picture of a Broadland scene and a montage encapsulating a head-and-shoulders photograph of the then FOND chairman Peter Brooks, who, in an interview, said of the *Voices* project: "If this can provide a better understanding and appreciation of local dialect, then it is to be welcomed. The BBC have been the worst offenders for portraying a Norfolk accent and creating the Mummerzet accent. So they should be congratulated now and we wish them well."

In the spring of 2007, FOND president **Professor Peter Trudgill** reported on two appearances he had made on BBC Radio Norfolk:

> A couple of time in recent weeks I have been invited to talk about the Norfolk dialect, and FOND, on BBC Radio Norfolk's afternoon show. One of the many people who rang in to make observations or ask questions suggested that it was not appropriate to talk about 'the Norfolk accent', because there is 'no such thing'. Actually, there are a number of different accents in Norfolk, not just one. And of course he had a point.
>
> I pointed out that the word 'accent' can be used to be as precise or vague as you like. Americans often say that I have a 'British accent'. Northerners might well say that we have a 'southern accent'. And people from the West Country might, if they are clever enough, recognise that we have an 'East Anglian accent'.
>
> But we would expect someone from Suffolk to say we have a 'Norfolk accent'. And it is quite true that, within Norfolk, people are able to tell the difference, at least sometimes, between accents from different parts of the county.
>
> It seems to me that I have only heard the pronunciation of hundred, naked, David as hundret, naket, Davet, in north Norfolk – is it found in the south too?
>
> I also suspect that never, together, as navver, togather are found mainly in the north – or am I wrong? And is towel pronounced as 'turl' a purely Norwich thing – or is it in rural areas as well?
>
> As I point out in my book, *The Norfolk Dialect*, some parts of

our county don't even really have a Norfolk accent at all. If I'm right – and please let me know if I'm not – it seems to me that speakers from places in the Norfolk Fens like Emneth, Upwell, West Walton, Outwell and the Walpoles have more of the sort of Cambridgeshire accent that you expect to hear in Wisbech.

Places like Clenchwarton, Terrington, Downham and the Tilneys, though, do have a Norfolk accent. It's also interesting that parts of north-eastern Suffolk have more of a Norfolk than Suffolk accent – Beccles, Bungay, Lowestoft and maybe even Southwold and Halesworth.

The point that most interested my caller, though, was the difference between Norwich and the country areas. He could have added Yarmouth and King's Lynn as well.

These urban areas all have accents distinctively different from those of the Norfolk countryside, although probably outsiders would not be able to hear this. And in fact the older Yarmouth accent was much more similar to the Norwich accent than it was to those of the rural areas in between.

Traditionally – it's less true these days – you could always spot a Norwich city person out in the countryside because he or she would drop their h's in a way that country people wouldn't. And Yarmouth people did the same.

FOND website's 72,000 'hits'

If the number of visitors to the Friends of Norfolk Dialect official website is anything to go by, the interest in our local vernacular appears to be on the increase, wrote **Ashley Gray** in his 'Mardle with the Editor' column in the winter 2008/09 edition of *The Merry Mawkin*. He went on:

The FOND website, set up by Pauline Dodd in March 2002, has recently attracted another 4,000 'hits' by visitors, bringing the total over the past seven years to over 72,000! Good news indeed and all down to Pauline's efforts, which are greatly appreciated.

With that number of people visiting the site – including

Norfolk exiles worldwide – for some it may be the only contact they have with us. If only they were to become members...!

One feature Pauline has included on the website is a guestbook, in which visitors may leave their comments or a short message. Those who do so are extremely complimentary, and pleased to have found us on the Internet.

The 'Ex-Pats' miss their homeland, it seems, some having lived abroad for a great many years and many are eager to relate happy times spent in our county, with a sincere love for the Norfolk dialect and sometimes used to good effect in their comments.

One such entry reads: "Tha's right nice ter know thar's a lot o' Norfolk people about still know how to talk the proper langwidge!"

Yis, my ole bewty, that that is, an 'orl! There're still Norfolk dumplins torkin' good ole Norfolk squit acrorse the length and breadth of our 'kingdom'.

CROMER AND NORTH NORFOLK DIALECT FESTIVAL

In April, 2008, FOND chairman Colin Burleigh was faced with the daunting prospect of succeeding Keith Skipper as adjudicator of the Cromer and North Norfolk Festival of Music, Drama and Dance dialect celebration. Keith had retired from this annual labour of love in 2007 after serving for an impressive 25 years.

"It was an entirely new thing for me to do, but I thrive on 'doing different'!" wrote Colin in the *Mawkin*. "Thankfully, I received several congratulations after the event, so perhaps I acquitted myself well. I look forward, should I be asked again, to doing likewise next year."

And he was and he did!

CHAPTER 40

The Boy Jimma: Tony Clarke 1937–2008

ALTHOUGH SOME OF US had known for a long time that Tony Clarke, FOND's first secretary and former chairman, was suffering from a terminal illness, it still came as a deep shock when Tony died on November 2, 2008, aged 71.

FOND chairman, Colin Burleigh, wrote in *The Merry Mawkin*:

"It was with much sadness that I learned of the death of Tony Clarke on November 2. We knew that Tony had been ill for some time but we marvelled at the fight he put up.

"He has served FOND very well, being a founder member and fulfilling the role of secretary, minutes secretary and vice-chairman, taking over as chairman for a short period before having to stand down because of ill health.

Tony Clarke: happy memories.

"The committee has happy memories of Tony lighting up our meetings and I'm sure all FOND members will never forget the annual pantomimes he wrote for us, bringing laughter into our lives on dull Sunday afternoons in January.

"Perhaps he was best known for his role as The Boy Jimma both with the Press Gang and at FOND-dews (his last being at Swanton Morley for the second visit by members of the East Lincolnshire Dialect Society, Far-Welter'd), when his laid-back routines always brought the house down."

The Boy Jimma, aka Tony Clarke!

Tony Clarke had written and produced a pantomime for FOND 'volunteers' to take part in every year at North Elmham Memorial Institute since 2001, and in January, 2009, the production was dedicated to Tony's memory. With the permission of his wife Pat, the script of *Cinderella*, one of his earliest contributions, was used again to good effect.

Tony was born at Attleborough. His father was a railwayman and, as recalled in one of Tony's books, *Mighta Bin Wuss*, had the bad luck to be stationmaster, successively, at Bungay and Watton when the passenger services to those towns closed down in 1953 and 1965.

His education included spells at Thetford and Bungay Grammar schools and he joined the then Norfolk News Company in 1954. His years as a journalist were spent in Norwich and Norfolk with Eastern Counties Newspapers (now Archant), a career interrupted only by his National Service in the RAF (1959–61) and a spell in Portsmouth as assistant editor of *Navy News* (1969–72).

Tony was chief reporter for 25 years at the company's branch office at Beccles where he and Pat were much involved in the community life of the Waveney Valley. They had a daughter and two sons.

Scholars and friends at Thetford Grammar School, 1953: Tony Clarke (top left) standing next to John Nickalls, publisher of Norfolk Dialect and its Friends.

CHAPTER 41

Lincs links reforged

IN THE WINTER 2008 edition of *The Merry Mawkin*, chairman **Colin Burleigh** reported on the second visit to Norfolk by the East Lincolnshire Dialect Society, Far-Welter'd, in September and FOND's second trip to Louth a month later:

> I'm happy to say I heard very good reports about the Far-Welter'd visit to Swanton Morley in September. My thanks must go to all the committee members who helped to make it a success, especially Ted Peachment, who handled the Village Hall booking, as well as the catering and running the entertainment.
>
> Special mention must also be made about Tony Clarke's Boy Jimma turn, as he'd lost none of his touch, although it was to be his final 'curtain call'.
>
> Our visit to Louth on October 24 was an occasion to savour, with eight of us making our way to Lincolnshire: myself and June, Tina and David Chamberlain, Ted Peachment, John Austrin, Norman Hart and Susan Palmer.
>
> The Mason's Arms was packed – thank heavens the Health and Safety officials were not about! – and our team of performers did their party pieces as usual.

Boy Jimma: his final curtain call.

Pictured during the FOND visit to Louth as guests of the Lincolnshire Dialect Society in October, 2008, are Dr Susan Palmer ('Star of the show', according to chairman Colin Burleigh) and Ted Peachment, from Swanton Morley.

John provided Boy John and Michael Brinded readings, Ted put across the story of the Creation in a manner (the Rev) Colin Riches would be proud of, and Tina's poems and jokes tickled the Louth folk's fancy!

I put over an excerpt from my 'stand-up' routine – but everyone agreed that the 'Star of the Show' was Susan Palmer. Her stream of anecdotes on her career as a doctor had the company in stitches – no pun intended – and everyone left the pub agreeing it was the best night out they'd had for years.

You may rest assured that our contingent did FOND proud.

CHAPTER 42

Short story competition

DURING THE SUMMER of 2008, Friends of Norfolk Dialect cast down the literary gauntlet by launching their prestigious Trosher Short Story Writing Competition.

Mawkin editor **Ashley Gray**, in his autumn editorial, wrote:

> The competition was inspired by the writings of our very own Norfolk lad, Keith Skipper, who, in his book, *How to Survive in Norfolk*, referred to the hope of resurrecting the 'Trosher Writing Competition' of bygone days, when joined-up writing was all the rage!
>
> In July, the good people at FOND, welcoming Keith's remarks regarding this little-known competition, came up with a modern-day set of rules and the result was the 'Trosher Short Story Writing Competition', which they unleashed among an unsuspecting public!
>
> So dew yew come on, tergether, an' git yar thinkin' caps on, huff the dust orf yar typewriters, an' start a-polishin' them there keys. 'Corse, blust me, we're all on us got a tearle tuh tell inside our hids, hen't we?

Entry forms were included in *The Merry Mawkin*. The competition was open to everyone regardless of age or nationality. First prize was £100, second £50 and third £30. Judges were FOND president Professor Peter Trudgill, chairman Colin Burleigh, secretary Peter Brooks and, of course, Keith Skipper.

The judges were kept extremely busy during November and December sorting through over 30 entries, with the first prize being

Memories of bygone days; to be lost forever by the horrors of war.

awarded to Jan Nicholls from Acle, for her moving story 'A Norfolk Heritage', a poignant tale of death and destruction during the Battle of Passchendaele in July, 1917.

The second prize was won by Mollie Bayfield from Clenchwarton, with her tale of a reminiscing telephone box, 'The Memory Box'.

In third place came Rose Agate from Fakenham, who wrote 'Foot Science', the story of an agricultural worker suffering from cold feet.

The prizes were presented at the 2009 AGM at North Elmham Memorial Institute in January by Keith Skipper, who said he was proud to follow such a literary luminary as Herbert Nathaniel Trosher – a Norfolk farmer and benefactor – who, in 1829, offered '10 good sovereigns for ten good chapters', with at least 20 pages of clear script legible joined-up writing which included some aspects of Norfolk life.

Colin Burleigh commented: "All the entries have been of a high standard and there is no doubt that this competition will be repeated next year and, hopefully, become a major project in FOND's calendar of events."

CHAPTER 43

FOND rests its case!

WRITING IN HIS 'Mardle with the Editor' column in the winter 2008 edition of *The Merry Mawkin*, **Ashley Gray** declared:

> It seems, from what I've heard, there'll be suffin' gorn about that we're likely to 'catch' early next year.
>
> Already thespians far and wide have hot-pedalled to the sensual delights of Market Shipborough, for the start of the next series of *Kingdom*. (Shooting has already begun, apparently – but tha's too good for some on 'em!)
>
> Picture, if you will, the daily routine. After an obligatory fry-up – with bewtiful Norfolk bearcon an'eggs, not to mention sossidges – the entire cast assemble under the Market Cross (or should I say *crorse*?) for 'ell-eee-cooshun' lessons!
>
> With any sense, they'd all be studying their individual copies of 'How Not to Make Norfolk People Cross'. You can but dream! But do the actors notice, or even care? Perhaps they'd be better placed advertising Mummerzet cider.
>
> The producers and scriptwriters of *Kingdom* must accept *some* responsibility as, in the first place, broad Norfolk has to be authentically written. These people fail to grasp that, in this county of ours, we have a unique way of saying things, not *always* in the order a 'furriner' might expect.
>
> We like to 'do-diffrunt', don't we? If the scriptwriters got *that* right, it would be a start.
>
> Perhaps it's the same with other television productions. Take *Heartbeat*, for instance, set in North Yorkshire. While Peggy Armstrong's accent *may* pass muster for viewers *elsewhere* in the

country, how does it really sound to folk born-and-bred in the North Riding?

Ashley Gray continued:

> I suppose I'm just as guilty, as many years ago while into amateur dramatics, I trod the boards in a role, once made famous by Brian Rix, for which a Yorkshire accent was called for.
>
> I fear I *may* have delivered my lines with the *merest* hint of 'Norfolk' creeping in – but at least the Sheringham audience understood me and laughed – or was it the loss of my trousers? I have no intention of repeating either, I hasten to add!

Does Stephen Fry really care about Norfolk...?
Why does he not insist on authentic local accents in his television series Kingdom? asks EDP reader Grace Parbury.

THE LAST WORD...
The last word on *Kingdom* and the Norfolk dialect goes to Eastern Daily Press reader Grace Parbury, of Sheringham, whose letter in the EDP on February 10, 2009, stated:

> *"If Stephen Fry cares so much for Norfolk (EDP January 31), why does he not insist on authentic local accents in his TV series Kingdom?*
>
> *"He must know what real Norfolk people sound like."*

FOND rests its case!

Merry Mawkin Miscellany

ON THE REMAINING PAGES is a selection of articles which have appeared in *The Merry Mawkin* over the past ten years. Where better to begin than with FOND's founder chairman, **Keith Skipper**? This was his contribution to the series 'What Norfolk Means to Me' in the spring edition of 2006:

Keith Skipper: 'Norfolk truly is everything to me.'

Skip's land with a mind of its own

Some say I've served a usual Norfolk apprenticeship. I was bred and born in the middle of the county at a time when big families (I was one of ten children) and small farms (over a dozen in our village) were in vogue. I became the first boy in the parish to pass the 11+, mainly because I was the first boy in the parish to have a pencil.

I caught the steam train to grammar school at Swaffham. By dint of hard work I mastered joined-up writing and lateral thinking by the time I reached puberty and so decided to become a famous journalist.

My first job, a foreign posting to Thetford, prepared me for 17 years of gleaning all the news that's fit to print, including several seasons as a Norwich City soccer scribe.

I swapped the pen for the microphone in 1980 as BBC Radio Norfolk hit the airwaves. I went stereo and married Diane three years later and moved to Cromer in the hope of finding someone older than me to talk to on the pier.

Our two sons underlined dangers inherent in reading Dickens as a bedtime story by christening me 'Aged P' long before they reached double figures.

For the past decade, aided by balmy breezes, I have mustered sufficient energy to pursue a freelance career as writer, broadcaster and entertainer. I helped set up Friends of Norfolk Dialect just before the end of the 20th century and so celebrated fulfilment of a long-cherished ambition to put support for this vital strand of our heritage on a formal footing.

I've written nearly thirty books and made several videos and CDs, all of them based on my specialist subject of Norfolk. It's been a delight to lead the Press Gang entertainers around local halls for over 20 years, all of them notable for recycling old but priceless material. I've mardled at hundreds of functions where a little squit can go a long way.

Norfolk truly is everything to me. A constant inspiration for my work, relaxation and family life. The only place I trust to make sense of a fast-changing world... by ignoring most of its blatant excesses.

Yes, I'll grow old gracefully in the land with a mind of its own.

Fond stalwart **Mike Coley**, from Northwold in west Norfolk, told the fascinating story of the Witch Tree in the *Mawkin's* autumn edition of 2003:

How Northwold's Witch Tree gave up the ghost

This particular witch, entirely natural and definitely not fashioned by human hand, is sadly no more.

She held court, albeit somewhat briefly, in my home village of Northwold, which can be found just off the A134, midway between King's Lynn and Thetford.

Her presence was brought to my attention by my aged aunt, from whose garden the photograph was taken.

Northwold, like so many of our old country places, has changed beyond recognition in recent years. I fear that it's no longer the self-contained community it once was, despite an increase in the population and, of course, in the number of dwellings needed to house them.

The Witch Tree at Northwold: It fell down two days after Mike Coley took this picture.

Today's homes are no longer interspersed with fields and meadows as were the houses of my youth. Instead they are tightly packed into every bit of space that at one time would have been considered inadequate, even for the age-old practice of cat swinging.

As a Ghost Buster myself (not my favourite title), I have always been aware of the abundance of supernatural energies that have existed in the village, and of the entities that have frequented the place.

I was therefore intrigued by

the Witch Tree, at first by the unique image it portrayed, of course, but afterwards by what followed a mere two days after the picture was taken.

After I had been drawn to take a snapshot of the tree in all its glory, within a couple of days it simply fell down.

Now I imagine that so striking an image, unless recreated by an expert in topiary, will be a long time in coming again.

But why did it appear in the first place? Was it chance or coincidence? Who knows? But if you ask me, it goes back to my earlier comments regarding the way that the old village has changed.

After all, sadly in my eyes, the small field you see in the foreground is itself marked down for development in the future, so I'm told.

The witch's appearance then and subsequent disappearance was an example of nature symbolically recognising that the character of the place, and thus the energies that exist there, have changed for ever.

To put it another way, when that tree fell down it was showing that the spirit of the past has simply given up the ghost.

The *Mawkin's* 'Norfolk by Adoption' series featured well-known people who, though not Norfolk-born, have made their permanent home here. In the autumn edition of 2003, the contributor was **Carol Bundock**, senior journalist with BBC TV in Norwich:

Why Carol intends to stay!

It snowed on June 2, 1975, and I remember this because it was the day I moved to Norfolk.

Driving along the A12 from my native Essex, the sleet and snow beat down on the windscreen, making me wonder if it was really true that Norfolk is always an overcoat colder than anywhere else.

Carol Bundock: 'I never intend to leave.'

But over the next few days the weather quickly changed into the beautiful summer of '75, and so began my love affair with Norfolk. Although to call it an affair suggests some fleeting passion, whereas the truth is much nearer a long and happy marriage.

I first lived in Holt, which was probably half the size it is now. The bypass hadn't been built, rabbits still frequented the old railway embankment, and there was no supermarket in the town.

But newly pregnant and with the luxury of time on my hands, I spent the summer exploring. The delights of the north Norfolk coast have stayed with me through the years, and as a family we all know the spot we refer to as 'our' patch on Stiffkey beach.

Winding lanes bowered by alexanders and chicory took me all over the county. I recall 'discovering' Baconsthorpe Castle one warm evening, and luxuriating in its beauty and seclusion. And as for the fish and chips at Cromer, well, need I say more!

As for the town of Holt itself, well it seemed to me idyllic... The sound of the Gresham's boys playing cricket on the field at the corner of Pearsons Road and the gentle ringing of St Andrew's bell, filling my garden nearby.

Over the years, as well as Holt, I've lived in South Creake, Corpusty and spent 12 years in the city too. We've now moved to the leafy suburbs of Thorpe St Andrew and it's comforting to have once more a parish church with the same name as the one in the Holt I came to love so much.

I'm proud, too, that Norfolk is the birthplace of both my children and that they still have strong ties with the county.

I owe much to the county professionally too. From being a mature student at UEA I went to work for BBC Radio Norfolk, and then on to *Look East*. I'm honoured to represent the county, too, as president of Girlguiding Norfolk.

Three years ago I covered a story about reed cutting on the Broads and after interviewing the renowned marshman Eric Edwards, asked him if after 25 years I counted as a local. He grunted a slightly begrudging "Yip," and I knew I'd properly arrived. And I never intend to leave.

In 2006 Carol was appointed a Deputy Lieutenant of Norfolk.

First contributor to the series 'What Norfolk Means to Me' in 2003 was the Lord Lieutenant of Norfolk, Sir Timothy Colman, a FOND vice-president (Chapter 13). Second was **James Hoseason**, a name synonymous with the Broads holiday industry and far beyond, also a FOND vice-president, and in 2003 he wrote:

Good nature, easy philosophy

Norfolk is special, very special. It is a proud, beautiful county with a distinguished history, populated by kind, friendly and highly individualistic people.

The region's abundance of seaside, waterside and countryside with wide-open skies, and Norfolk's special daylight, provide many of the county's richest features. But it is the very individualistic character of so many of the inhabitants that makes up much of the county's distinctiveness.

James Hoseason: 'Kind, friendly, highly individualistic people.'

Maybe it is to do with having to possess the ability to stand up to the bitter cold and wind-strength of Norfolk's mid-winter nor'-easters that helps mould the 'do different' character.

That particular stubbornness means, for example, that when pressure is put on for a change or 'improvement' (and particularly when it comes from outside the region) it is often destined for intense opposition. A most worthy characteristic.

The Norfolkman is greatly skilled. And he has a rare ability for inventiveness. He is not afraid to develop new methods and new materials, but he doesn't take kindly to being told to do so by 'foreigners'.

He knows how to use all the elements, particularly the weather, to his advantage. So much of the region's economy and also its recreational opportunities turn on the skilful use of wind-and-water by and on the sea and on the waterways and by the county's plentiful heathland.

It is fascinating, isn't it, that history seems to be about to repeat itself with the planned introduction of offshore windmills to provide energy for the region. So similar in many ways to the windmills and windpumps that harnessed vital wind-energy for pumping and mill-grinding purposes here 150 years ago.

The Norfolkman has for centuries learned to further hone his great skills in the essential techniques of caring for the land using the weather to his fullest vantage in every detail. The success of the size and diversity of the region's range of crops and stock are a matter of great pride to the county.

The good nature and the easy philosophy of the Norfolk folk have always been a feature of visitors' comments. And they are right to feature this oh-so-important characteristic.

Where else in the world would a local garage owner display this note in his window a few weeks before Christmas: "A happy Christmas to all my customers wot hev paid their bills, and a prosperous New Year to them wot hent"?

"Discreet not boastful." "Confident not brash."

That was how our Continental visitors viewed the Norfolkman as he went about his duties. They were so right. I have always treasured the sheer perception of those observations.

Two long-serving members of the FOND committee recalled their memories of growing up in rural Norfolk in a series of articles in *The Merry Mawkin*. **Janet Woodhouse** has been treasurer of FOND throughout the ten years of the organisation's existence. **Jean Eaglen**, of Hingham, a committee member since 2002, has been responsible for making a number of dialect tape recordings within the community and has also been involved with the FOND schools project. In the summer 2003 edition of the *Mawkin*, Janet recalled her childhood at North Elmham in the 1940s and 1950s:

When boys dived off main-road bridge into the river

By Janet Woodhouse

I always had to go to Sunday school at church. Most of my friends went to the Methodist Sunday school where they had concerts, with recitations.

I didn't know what recitations were but thought they must be good. My grandmother always said, "We don't go to chapel," and sadly I never got to find out what a recitation was! I did enjoy the festivals at church, though. I loved picking primroses for Easter decorations in church, and covering the steps of the Children's Corner with moss and watering it all and watching fascinated as the water rushed along the floor and we flicked it into the gratings over the hot pipes.

Janet Woodhouse (née Yarham), aged six: Treat of the week – going to the pictures in the village hall on a Saturday night!

At harvest festival time we got in the way trying to help putting out vegetables and fruit – we really only wanted to eat the apples if we could.

At Christmas we gathered holly for decorations in church and we used to fight to see who could put the figures of the Nativity in the crib; they were chipped even then.

When we were children we always seemed to be outside. If you wanted someone to play with, you just wandered around the village until someone else joined you, then off you would go.

In summer a popular place was the Billingford bridge (blown up for safety reasons in 1954) where everyone would paddle and learn to swim.

Daring boys would dive off the hump-backed bridge down into the river below.

I cannot recall anyone ever being hurt doing that, but what a hue and cry there would be today if children were caught diving off a bridge on a main road into a muddy river!

The treat of the week would be to go to the Institute (village hall) on a Saturday night for the pictures. A short film would be followed by a longer one, brought out from Dereham. All the bikes would be lined up outside, as very few people had cars and anyway cars weren't got out for short journeys.

Fetes and jumble sales were all good for entertainment and eagerly looked forward to, as well as weddings. I can't remember how we knew when there was going to be a wedding but we'd all go up to the church to watch the event.

The door facing the road was the way into church, so we children could quite legitimately dodge around on the roadside, getting in everyone's way to have a good look and hopefully wangle an invitation to the reception!

Slugs and dodmans in the well water!

By Jean Eaglen

My first memories are of my father going to war in 1940. I remember the snow was very deep on February 6 as we left to catch the big double-decker bus. We had no idea what was happening!

With three small children to look after, it was a very hard life for my mother. As I was the oldest, aged four, I had to help her with the chores. I can just see the big galvanised bucket coming up from the well outside our back door. Often it had slugs and dodmans in it. Mother would just throw them out and we used the water for everything. Even our toilet was up the garden — bucket and chuck it – with little squares of newspaper hanging on the wall. The bucket had to be emptied weekly by my poor mother – on to the garden, I believe, but we did have some lovely tomatoes!

Jean Eaglen (née Blyth), aged 11: 'I screamed and ran indoors...'

There was no night (honey) cart to collect. One visit was very scary for me. I think I must have been about six. As I'd come home from school – over a mile away – and before dark we were all sent up to the lavatory. It was almost dark in the little shed and I reached for my paper square. I screamed and ran indoors, telling my mother there was a rat in there. She found my brother's pet rabbit had escaped and was sitting in the corner. As it was a two-holer, it was lucky for the rabbit that there was a lid on the large seat. I do hope you're not eating your meal while reading this!

Between 2001 and 2006, Norfolk antiquary and book-collector **Ron Fiske** wrote a popular series of fourteen articles for *The Merry Mawkin*, 'The Norfolk Dialect: Guides to Reading and Research'. In 1893, the *Eastern Daily Press* published a booklet entitled *Broad Norfolk*, including a list of nearly 700 dialect words. In 1949 the *EDP* produced another book with the same title, a compilation of letters written by *EDP* readers. In the winter *Mawkin* of 2006, Ron Fiske wrote of a third book, again entitled *Broad Norfolk*, the work of the *EDP's* distinguished writer Eric Fowler, aka essayist Jonathan Mardle:

Ron Fiske: Norfolk antiquary and book-collector.

Recording is vital as lessening of dialect accelerates in age of texting

Broad Norfolk: by Jonathan Mardle, Wensum Books.

In the last two articles in this series we have dealt with books entitled *Broad Norfolk*.

Even so, a third with the same title appeared in 1973. Written by Eric Fowler, under his well-known pseudonym, Jonathan Mardle, it was published by Wensum Books under the guiding hands of George Nobbs and Alan Dean. It was aided by the drawings of Joe Lee, a political cartoonist with the London *Evening News* and, in his retirement, with the *Eastern Daily Press*.

His drawing of 'Jonathan...

mardling' is a treasured glimpse of Eric, forced to endure a substitute for his favourite sport of bowling.

Eric's *Broad Norfolk* adopted a new format: a wide-ranging discourse split into seven chapters covering the language, sounds, words and manner of speaking before concluding with some well-known place-name renderings, a few of his stories and useful glossary.

'Jonathan... mardling' is Joe Lee's caption for his cartoon of Eric Fowler.

He carried well the double-edged sword of journalism. His natural gifts had been honed to make his writing readably attractive while preserving the restraints of timetable and deadline.The best of these traits resulted in a very entertaining book, one that proved so popular it called for three more printings.

Eric reminds us that, in general, accounts of East Anglian dialect were written by the squire, who liked to chuckle over it, the parson, who found it etymologically interesting, or the doctor who found it quaint. He even tells a story against himself. When talking to another journalist he used the word 'fulfer' and was immediately asked where he had learned the word. Eric replied that he had first heard it when he was about eight years old from a boy who helped in his father's garden.

"Grr!" his colleague remarked. "I can speak better Norfolk than you can. You see I was a gardener's boy."

In other words, while he mixed with all sorts of people, he was bound by the restraints of standards of English.

One example of this occurs in his chapter 'The Manner of Speaking'. Dealing with 'what grammarians call the historic present', he relates the sort of comment which is often made to somebody who thinks he has made a bargain: "I reckon he see yew a-comin'."

The 'reckon' is too good and does not fall well from a Norfolk working class tongue. "He must'a see yew a-comin," would be more likely although, sad to say, 30 years after Eric wrote, "He must'a seen yew a-comin'," would be more likely.

It is probably unfair to make such selective criticism, but it does illustrate how quickly local speech is being debased. This aspect is covered in Fowler's final chapter, 'Can Broad Norfolk Survive?'. In it he shares Dr Joseph Wright's views, written in 1904, in his *English Dialect Grammar and English Dialect Dictionary* 'that pure dialect speech is rapidly disappearing even in country districts, owing to the spread of information and to modern facilities in intercommunication.'

Like him, Eric Fowler knew that 'the dialect that even old country-folk speak today (1973) is not quite the same language as their grandparents spoke'. But he was not nostalgic for the sake of it and felt uncomfortable when people talked of 'preserving broad Norfolk'.

He sadly, and perhaps surprisingly, questioned whether 'when a dialect becomes so self-conscious it can possibly remain a genuine dialect and not an affectation'.

He is probably right, for the lessening of dialect in Norfolk's tongue has quickened more in the 33 years since he wrote than during the previous 70 years since Dr Wright wrote. This is bound to accelerate in an age when 'texting' relies on abbreviation, and silly slogans replace proper language. Despite what he says, the language ought to be recorded even if it becomes more historical.

Wally Webb is one of BBC Radio Norfolk's best-known and longest-serving presenters, broadcasting weekdays his own programme from 4am to 6.30am and then, till 9am, becoming a roving reporter from virtually anywhere in the county wherever a news story takes him.

In the winter 2003 edition of *The Merry Mawkin* he contributed to the 'Norfolk by Adoption' series:

How Wally took the right road

"Strit orn," said the little old lady. I'd stopped to ask the way to Coltishall. "Strit orn an' yule see the sign."

My initiation into the Norfolk dialect had begun. So I kept

straight on down the North Walsham road until I saw the sign for RAF Coltishall.

It was my first day in the county, but little did I know how much I would grow to love the place, the people and the lifestyle. Even before I left the RAF at the start of 1980 I'd travelled many roads with my mobile disco, broadcasting every Sunday on Hospital Radio Norwich and spent many late nights as a DJ in Scamps Nightclub.

Wally Webb: 'Don't tell too many people about it!'

Fate took control then and, when it seemed I'd have to look elsewhere for employment in radio, the BBC gave me the chance to stay on. Through a weekly documentary called *Village Voice*, I spent seven years paying a weekly visit to a different Norfolk community. My weekly travels to sometimes remote communities led me to appreciate the beauty and tranquillity of the county. Rugged and unpredictable shorelines, unexpectedly stunning vistas just around a bend in a country lane. It also taught me much about the folk of Norfolk. Meeting many of them on home ground – in their homes – and hearing at first hand their own stories of life over the decades.

Before long I discovered another beauty. The Broads. I guess from the first moment I unhitched the mooring rope and drifted into its watery solitude I was smitten. Every opportunity was seized to escape to this other planet and not long after I was to meet the Norfolk girl who would come to share it with me.

Subsequently we bought a bigger boat and love nothing more than casting off for a few days down the Chet to Loddon or dropping the mudweight in the middle of Salhouse Broad on one of those summer evenings when the paddle steamer comes gliding round with the music of the jazz band lighting up the evening atmosphere.

Sheri and I were married in 1989 and since then she's tried to teach me Norfolk. But it's not so much the dialect (which I'm hopeless at imitating anyway) but the way things are expressed.

I always remember during the *Village Voice* years being told by the chairman of such-and-such parish council that there were 368 people on the *electrical* roll. It was a while before I caught on, but when Sheri tells me there's a knock on the doorbell – well!

That's just one of dozens of virtues about Norfolk. I wouldn't shout about them too loudly, though. Over the years I've larnt to dew wot Norfik people do. Be good to the people, don't abuse the natural beauty on our doorstep and don't tell too many people about it, 'cos otherwise they'll orl wanta cum here!

'What Norfolk means to me' – in which well-known Norfolk people express their thoughts on what makes their home county special to them. In the *Mawkin's* summer 2006 edition, **Neil Storey**, historian, author, academic lecturer, one of the most popular speakers in the county, and life-member of FOND, explained why Norfolk is an integral part of his identity:

Identity formed from a unique history, language and culture

I was born a historian; I had to be, growing up in a house shared with grandparents who related tales and memories in everyday conversation. I had to pick up some of the stories of people, places and notable events from their past or I would have had no idea what my grandparents or their friends were talking about.

I was inspired and encouraged by retired history teacher, Mary McManus, to put together my first talks on the history of my home town, when I was about 14.

Having seen 'the boy done good' with my talks, a few folks

Neil Storey: FOND life member, 'a born historian'.

joked, "You ought to write a book." One of them, the late Terry Davy, of Dereham, even said, "I'll publish it."

So with honest guidance from Terry I set about writing my first tome on a rickety old manual typewriter.

Each book has explored a different aspect of the history of our county and city, the people and Norfolk way of life. I hope, with God and readership willing, I shall always write books on my beloved county.

Over the years it has truly been a privilege and pleasure to meet many of the people who have been part of the fabric of our county. The stories they have shared have enriched my books, made us laugh and moved us to tears.

The fortitude, bravery and reticence of many county folk who have done extraordinary deeds or acts of compassion in times of peace, war and disaster mark the character of true Norfolk people.

I love my home county and take pride in finding my family name dotted over the pages of Norfolk history for hundreds of years. I feel a deep sense of belonging here, it is an integral part of my identity – an ethnic identity formed from our unique history, language and culture that should be respected as much as any other.

I concur with Nelson and will always declare: "I am a Norfolk man, and glory in being so."

On September 23, 1993, my wife Shelagh and I were lucky enough to be among a group of 130 people who set off from Norwich to travel east-to-west round the world in 23 days. It was organised by BBC Radio Norfolk, led by presenter **Roy Waller** and tour manager Andy Garside, and accompanied by Roy's wife and Radio Norfolk producer Sylvie, together with the station's Wally Webb and Peter Glanville and his wife Cath. We travelled via Hongkong, Cairns, Sydney, Fiji and Hawaii – a total of 23,000 miles and the adventure was an unqualified success. So successful that three years later 57 of us, again led by Roy and Sylvie, plus tour manager John Russell, circumnavigated the globe once more, this time west-to-east via New Zealand, Bali and Bangkok.

Roy Waller: Sheriff of Norwich, aka BBC Radio Norfolk presenter!

Two great and highly successful expeditions and it's not surprising that both Roy Waller and Wally Webb were among those I asked to contribute to *The Merry Mawkin*. Roy presents his radio programme each weekday afternoon and a country music show on Saturdays. For many years he also commentated on Norwich City football matches. Following in the earlier footsteps of Bryan Gunn, he served as Sheriff of Norwich for the year 2008–2009.

In the spring of 2002, he wrote in the *Mawkin*:

Roy Waller – a good old Norfolk boy!

It's been mentioned many times when I'm on the radio that I have a Norfolk accent. Well, I make no excuse for that.

After all, I'm proud that Norfolk is my home county and Norwich my home city.

It's a good life working for BBC Radio Norfolk. No two days are ever the same. It's enabled me to go round the world twice, meet many famous people and be 'gunged' on the *Noel Edmunds Show*. Glamorous? Well yes, but I still try to remember my roots and the fact that I'm a good old Norfolk boy.

As recalled in Chapter 3, **Martin Kirby**, FOND's then vice-chairman and newly-appointed editor of *The Merry Mawkin*, announced that he and his family would be emigrating to Spain in 2001 to run an organic farm in Catalonia. The move was to prove a successful one for the ex-*Eastern Daily Press* deputy editor and in the 2002 summer/autumn edition of the *Mawkin*, Martin wrote:

Thas a small world: Catalonia and the Norfolk connection

Blas' bor, thas a small world.

As a few of you may know, I somehow found a good reason to forsake adorable Norfolk after 42 years, seduced by the notion of a wholly different life halfway up a Catalan mountain in north-east Spain.

And I can't say it's been easy leaving behind my home county and our families (even if it's been glorious to change the rhythm of our lives and for Maggie and me to find a great deal more time for ourselves and the children). The old joke at the *EDP* office was that I was nailed to the floor, the resident Norfolk codger with 'I'll never go!' tattooed across my chest.

But off we went, not so much into the sunset but an arctic squall on a bleak January night 18 months ago.

So how different is it? Well, we potter around the lanes, wave to the old boys sitting on benches watching the world go by, have a mardle in the shop, drift around the market on a Tuesday, and curse at any changes that may 'develop' this glorious, peaceful backwater. Sounds familiar?

The biggest worry is the new road across the mountains which

Down on their farm in Catalonia: Martin Kirby and his wife Maggie Whitman with children Joe Joe and Ella.

means, heaven forbid, that second-homeowners from Barcelona and even abroad may target local properties.

But it's a thousand miles away from my homeland and you wouldn't think Norfolk, or should I say Friends of Norfolk Dialect, would come up in conversation. I'm having enough trouble grappling with the Catalan dialect. Yet I never cease to be amazed by the size of our planet and how life can twist and turn like the road from Saxthorpe to Matlaske.

We count a few English people among our many new friends and one is Rachel, an apprentice master glass craftswoman (try saying that without your teeth in) who lives in Barcelona but is engaged to a man from our rural neck of the woods.

One weekend she rang to say she'd like to call by with a friend who was staying with her. We were planning one of our usual riotous supper parties and invited them to join us.

They duly arrived and we were introduced to a lovely lady who spoke English extremely well but with an indefinable accent. "Are you Catalan or Spanish?" I asked. "Oh no," she replied. "I'm from Switzerland."

"I only know one person in Switzerland," I said. "Two now," she smiled, "but who is the other one?"

"Professor Peter Trudgill at the University of Fribourg."

"I know Peter very well," she said. " I studied with him."

Cor, what a rumm'n. I thought I'd detected a slight Norfolk melody in her accent…..

Vera Youngman has been a valued member of the FOND committee from the beginning and it was her home, Forge House, Yaxham, near Dereham where members met regularly for ten years and enjoyed scrumptious cakes and tea afterwards.

In 2002 Vera was presented with a Certificate of Excellence for 20 years of devoted work with Victim Support, and similar thanks and recognition from Norfolk Constabulary 'for your service to the Victims of Crime'. Tribute to 'Our Vera – a special, caring kind of person' was paid by treasurer Janet Woodhouse in *The Merry Mawkin* at the time, and it was in the spring edition of 2006 that Vera Youngman told the story behind the international success of the Norfolk show jumper, Sunsalve, who achieved equestrian fame at the Olympic Games in Rome:

Sunsalve – a true Norfolk hero

This is the true story of a very remarkable horse, born at High House, Shipdham, near Dereham, bred and owned by a real Norfolk man, Oliver Anderson.

My interest in the animal came through my father, Robert Charles Andrews, who was not only a Norfolk man but the village farrier at Yaxham from 1910. He was known generally as Charlie and I am his youngest daughter.

Elizabeth Anderson and Sunsalve in action at White City. (Right) Sunsalve being shod in 1961 by 80-year-old Yaxham farrier, Charlie Andrews.

Vera Youngman, 84, in 2006 with Sunsalve's preserved hoof.

Sunsalve had something of a charmed life. As a foal, he injured a hock which could have put paid to his chances of a successful life.

Mr Anderson consulted my father, who, after wracking his brain, asked for Mr Anderson's permission to shoe the young horse with a specially built-up half-shoe. The owner agreed and the animal was thus shod for his first winter.

Eventually, the leg straightened and Sunsalve went on to become a famous show jumper. Ridden originally by the owner's daughter, Elizabeth, he won the Queen Elizabeth Cup.

After an unfortunate split in the family, Sunsalve was ridden by several other riders, including Pat Smythe. Pat was one rider who did not get on too well with the horse, thinking that he had a defect in his feet, although this was not so. Later he was ridden by David Broome, who won a bronze medal on Sunsalve in the Rome Olympics and eventually the King George V Gold Cup.

This was a remarkable record, one that as far as I know has never been equalled, because the Elizabeth Cup is for lady riders and the King George is for gentlemen riders.

I feel that Sunsalve's story should be more widely known in the county, having been born and bred in Norfolk, owned by a Norfolk man and shod by a Norfolk blacksmith, and this makes him a true Norfolk hero.

Sunsalve's last rider was Tony Holden from Norwich, but unfortunately the horse suffered a heart attack while exercising at Shipdham and died on June 22, 1962.

My father and I then went to the knackers' yard in Fakenham to retrieve Sunsalve's two front legs so that Dad could prove the horse had no disease in his feet. They turned out to be perfect. We had them preserved and I have one and Mr Anderson had the other.

I would love to talk to anyone who might wish to find out more about this magnificent beast which owed his life to the expertise of my dear old Dad.

For some 23 years, **Charles** and **Joy Boldero** have 'written walks' in the *Eastern Daily Press* and other publications and produced numerous books to guide ramblers along the footpaths of our countryside. In 2006, during my final year of editorship of the *Mawkin*, Shelagh and I enjoyed Joy and Charles's hospitality at their lovely home in north Norfolk, where Charles kindly undertook the printing and distribution of the newsletter.

In the series 'Norfolk by Adoption', they contributed this piece for the spring edition of *The Merry Mawkin* in 2006:

You've made us so welcome!

In 1980 Charles took early retirement. We were very much involved in the Somerset area where we lived. We ran a large horse show, chaired a range of activities, including Friends of the local hospital, Civic Society, plus a lot more.

Charles and Joy Boldero with Tammy: 'Norfolk folk are caring and friendly.'

Also, we took a leading part in the village we lived in. It was once a small rural parish of about 500 folk. Then the M5 came through and the village when we left was 2,000-odd and growing. We wanted a rural county to retire to, but where?

Then the invitation arrived, a cousin's 40th wedding anniversary. They lived, and still do, in Hunstanton. Where we had booked in, the landlord and his wife were far from welcoming, so we, in the dark, wandered the country lanes and found Blickling. It still amazes us how we did so! There at the Buckinghamshire Arms we received a royal welcome.

The following year we went back for a long weekend and had a good look at Norfolk. We are country folk from head to toe, as our forefathers were before us.

By late 1983 we had moved to Norfolk and were living on the outskirts of Stibbard. Soon there was a knock at the door – a Mr Daniels from the village with an armful of vegetables. "Just call in if you would like more," he said.

Christmas morning we walked to church. Teenagers on cycles were riding hell-for-leather on the pavement – they jumped off their cycles and shouted, "Happy Christmas!" A year later we were able to move to the house we had first wanted in Thurning.

We found that Norfolk folk were caring and friendly, they do not waste their money either, nor yours. We helped at the Briston Centre under the auspices of Mrs Meanley. One day she said to us, "You like walking, well Robert Christy is retiring from writing walks for the *EDP*. Ring Michael Pollitt."

We did so and he asked us to send in a walk. That was in 1986 and we are still writing walks for the *EDP* and now also the *Let's Talk!* and *Norfolk Afloat* magazines. Norfolk is not flat, it has many attractive faces and nooks and crannies.

The villages are full of historic content, especially if you take time to talk to the 'locals'. That is what is so nice about Norfolk; people still have the time to say, "Hello, how are you?"

We have not regretted one moment of moving to Norfolk, and that is due to the Norfolk folk who have made us so welcome. Worries, yes – those who do not understand 'rural' have no idea nor want to do so. They do not understand small, caring communities. 'Big brother' only knows 'huge', with folk becoming just a number, no longer a person; individuality not allowed.

Norfolk folk are used to having to fight for their corner. It started with the Vikings centuries ago. Now it is confession time. In about 800AD or so the Bolderos landed on the Suffolk shores in their long boats! However – Joy is a Celt. Welsh, and very proud of being so!

Dr William Woods, director, Dutch and Flemish Studies Centre, St Mary the Less, Norwich, has written a number of dialectal articles for *The Merry Mawkin* over the years. This one appeared in the spring edition in 2006 and would no doubt have been of particular interest to readers in the Waveney Valley where the old pub game of dwile-flonking (*see page 185*) was revived a few decades ago:

Dwile? Dew yew look for it in Dutch!

It is said that some people wrap dwiles around their feet to clean the floor. The housewife kneeling in front of her doorstep to rub it with a dwile and elbow grease is a typical image.

Barmen use dwiles to mop up spilt drinks. Opinions differ as to what a dwile may be used for and what form it takes, but it is one of the most familiar Norfolk and Suffolk dialect words.

Commonly a dwile is a floorcloth, but it could be used for cleaning walls, doors, windows or any household surface. It could be fixed to the end of a stick as a mop or wrapped around the end of a broom or squeegee.

It might be made of wool, cotton or leather, it might be a specially manufactured coarse cleaning cloth, or an old vest, flannel or tea towel. Usually it is a damp cloth as opposed to a duster or rag.

There is an easy way to clarify the definition of a dwile because an almost identical word exists in standard Dutch and it is directly from Dutch that the Norfolk word derives.

Many Norfolk dialect words are similar to Dutch words, but often this is a result of parallel descent from Anglo-Saxon and North Sea Germanic, so that the similarity is coincidental and Dutch influence difficult to prove.

In the case of dwile, the earliest record in English is of 19th century use in East Anglia, whereas the Dutch *dweil* is recorded in Middle Dutch and so has come across to Norfolk from Holland, where it is a common word.

Here is a translation of Van Dale's *Modern Dutch Dictionary* definition of the word *dweil*: woollen or coarse linen thick cloth with which moisture is removed from floor (doorstep, etc), or which when dampened is used to remove dirt: swab.

There is also a verb *dweilen*: remove with a dwile, or clean.

A couple of early 20th century definitions can be found in the great *Woordenboek der Nederlandsche Taal* (Dictionary of the Dutch Language): piece of material, now usually of coarse flannel, used to clean floors, to remove moisture or dirt or for similar work, or, bundle of rags nailed to a stick, in particular used in cleaning on ships: swab.

For *dweilen* the *WNT* has: wipe off with a cloth, and, clean or dry with a dwile.

English dictionary definitions concur, but less precisely. *The Oxford English Dictionary* lists *dwile* as a dialect word for a house-flannel, floorcloth or mop and quotes East Anglian examples of Moor (1823) – towel; Forby (1825) – mop of refuse wool, coarse rubbing rug; and Suffling (1887) – dishcloth. Keith Skipper (1996) and Robert Malster (1999) both settle for floorcloth.

So to get a good clear detailed picture of what a *dwile* is, the place to look is in Dutch.

I first met **John Timpson** in the mid-1950s when we were reporters covering local events for rival newspapers in north Norfolk. He was with the *Eastern Daily Press* and the *Dereham and Fakenham Times* and I worked for the *Norfolk Chronicle*.

Later we would travel together in his car to report on district council meetings and later still I was to join him on the *EDP*, before he left Norfolk for the BBC to find fame on both television and radio. John became the corporation's royal correspondent, reporting on a number of royal tours overseas, and a TV newsreader before becoming a presenter on the Radio 4 flagship morning programme, *Today*. He retired to Norfolk, became a best-selling author, and in 2002 he agreed to write a piece for *The Merry Mawkin* in the 'Norfolk by Adoption' series. He was a member of FOND.

Daydream that materialised

John Timpson: extolling the delights of Norfolk.

When Pat and I first moved to Norfolk as newly-weds, 51 years ago, our families and friends thought we were quite mad. To them, East Anglia was just a flat expanse of nothing in particular except for the occasional windmill and a permanent Arctic wind, a cross between Siberia and the Zuider Zee.

I confess I had much the same picture. My two previous excursions to Norfolk had not been very encouraging. One was a family holiday with my parents at Cromer, when it rained continuously and the only entertainment was watching the fire brigade pump out the hotel basement. The other was as a National Serviceman during the bitter winter of 1947, when I spent six miserable weeks in a wooden hut somewhere in Thetford Forest.

Predictably, the Army managed to run out of fuel and we could only warm the hut by burning the chairs, the tables and even the spare beds. We were working our way through the roof joists when we were finally dispatched to the comparative cosiness of the Austrian Alps.

It was the chance of a reporting job in Dereham that brought me back in 1951 – and alas, the weather had not improved. There was rarely a winter when the lanes were not blocked by snow, and in our pantry at North Elmham the pickled onions froze in the vinegar and the eggs solidified and burst their shells.

The sanitation system was a bucket down the garden, the water supply was hand-pumped from a well by the back door, and on washdays we lit a fire under the copper in the wash-house to heat the water. But during those early years we developed an affection for Norfolk which has stayed with us ever since.

When the BBC job in London came along in 1959 and we reluctantly went back 'down south', we kept in touch with our Norfolk friends, we came back as often as we could, and I shamelessly extolled the delights of Norfolk whenever the chance arose – much to the irritation, I suspect, of my fellow broadcasters, and certainly to the embarrassment of some of my Norfolk friends. "Don't keep on about it," they pleaded, "or we'll be getting everybody coming here...."

For nearly three decades, as the Home Counties became more and more congested and the daily battle with the London rat-race became more and more tedious, we promised that one day we would return to Norfolk – permanently. Not every day-dream materialises, but happily this is one that did. I know we shall always be incomers, but we still feel as though we've come home.

John Timpson died in Norfolk in November, 2005, aged 77.

Former *Eastern Daily Press* reporter **Anthony Grey** himself made international headlines in the 1960s when, as Reuters' correspondent in Peking, he fell foul of the Chinese cultural revolution and spent two years in solitary confinement. After his release, Tony wrote a book on his experiences, *Hostage in Peking*, and a series of best-selling novels. He returned to his Norfolk base to develop his own publishing business, The Tagman Press.

In March, 2002, Tony joined us at a FOND-dew in the Lophams' Village Hall in south Norfolk and not only was it a reunion with his old *EDP* colleagues, Keith Skipper, Tony Clarke, Peter Mallett and myself, but also with friends and acquaintances made when he worked at the *EDP's* Diss office.

During his talk, Tony mixed mardling with melody as he sang a Norfolk song specially composed for the occasion to the tune of the Charlie Chaplin hit, *Smile*.

Dwile

Dwile flonking, the pub game revived in the Waveney Valley in the 1960s.

Use a dwile
If you spill some humous
With olive oil
Down yar Aunty's bloomers
As they dry by her fire
That'll soon soothe her ire.

Or if you slop
Half a jar of piccalilli
Down the front o' yar trousers
And feel pertickularly silly,
You'll soon see yar neighbours
Start to smile,
If you flash yar dwile...
So if any form of spillage badness
Drives you to the brink of madness
Be it tea, milk or beer,
Or somethin' warse,
Never fear!

That's the time
You must keep on wipin'
Dwile! What's the use o' gripin'
Yar life will never be a trial
If you use yar dwile.

© Copyright – All rights reserved by FOND and the landlord of the pub near Stratton Strawless, who wishes to remain anonymous.

[Original lyrics of a well-known song that, according to Anthony Grey, keen supporter of FOND, was rescued by him from an ancient beer-stained music case along with a mouldy, smelly dwile, all discovered in an old piano stole near Stratton Strawless, Norfolk]

'Sheringham Seafront' by Norfolk artist Vaughn Limmer (top right); 'The Quiet Fishermen' written specially for The Merry Mawkin in 2003 by Norfolk poet and former EDP journalist Tim Lenton (lower right).

The Quiet Fishermen

Sea to sea
your dark eyes swallow the tides
as sand shapes your faces.

You stand defence
against the deep
riding now and now the wild white horse
that leaps to throw you,

stealing a meal from between
the feet of the dragon.

Against the splintering sky
you fix your fragile chariot,
pulling the magic wood through wind and water
steering towards God

then stand and wait.
Smoke rises:
the night is cool.

Stillness becomes you.
Touching eternity
needs a steady hand.

'Norfolk by Adoption': **Penelope Ann Seligman**, OBE, JP, DL – universally known as '**Paddy**'. She has been closely connected with virtually all forms of public order activities. She is a JP, chairman of NORCAS with its role in combating drug and alcohol abuse, chairman of the County Domestic Violence Forum , trustee and chairman of the Project Group of Norwich PACT (Partners Against Crime Taskforce) and has worked in four prisons – Feltham Young Offenders Institution, Wayland, Norwich and Whitemoor; a member of the Board of Visitors and is currently a mental health hospital manager at Rowan House. She is chairman of the *EDP* 'We Care' Appeal and it is this role which has endeared her to members of FOND.

From the *Mawkin*, 2005:

Your kindness, generosity know no bounds!

In choosing to adopt Norfolk I have returned to an area that I fell in love with long ago. Happy childhood summer holidays spent in what we call the Sea House at Holme was my induction to Norfolk. Wall to wall sunshine every day from dawn to dusk – swimming the ponies in the sea, shrimping and dragging for dabs. Why didn't we discover Sea Henge all those years ago?

And then with my own children growing up in London, we decided to buy a cottage somewhere safe so we could escape at weekends – yes, we were second-home owners for five years in Thursford, where wonderful George Cushing would appear on a Friday night with a box of vegetables or a bag of mussels and sit for a mardle.

Paddy Seligman: 'Everyone made us welcome.'

Everyone made us welcome – the local sergeant would drop in for a chat and Sydney came by for a game of draughts. He always won!

So when Anthony began to plan for retirement there was only one place to be. We wanted something in north Norfolk and were lucky to hear about Valley Farm House before it came on the market. We moved from London in July, 1987. The house needed a bit of work doing on it and the garden was a wilderness. Harry and Bernard 'watched' us for a while – several weeks – and then asked if we could do with a bit of help. Readily accepted.

I found them hard to understand to begin with. Bernard, born and reared in Gunthorpe, only left the village to go to war. His mother locked the front door as he left and didn't open it again until he came back. He had been a prisoner of the Japanese.

Bernard and Harry became firm friends and continued to help us until old age took its toll and I was honoured when asked to present the eulogy at Bernard's funeral.

The scrub in the meadow at the back of the house was going to be a challenge to clear, but when we returned from a holiday in 1988 the farm manager had sent his men to clear it all for us and, a few weeks later, Robin turned up with a couple of Hebridean sheep in the back of the Land-Rover, threw them out and told us they were just what we needed to keep the grass down. We still have their descendants!

The kindness and generosity of people have known no bounds. The pace of life in Norfolk was certainly pleasantly slower than London, although I don't find that now – almost 20 years on!

Having been a magistrate in London, I wanted to carry on and was appointed to the Norwich Bench. Looking back at a piece I did for the Camberwell newsletter in 1989, I see that I found the standard of crime no lower than London and that I had to upgrade my 'tariff', the sentences in Norwich being quite a bit heavier than Camberwell. I also found that male members of the bench more readily accepted women in the chair and that the CPS lawyers were, on the whole, superior to those in London.

I have immersed myself into Norfolk life in many fields but the one dearest to my heart is the *EDP* 'We Care' Appeal. So many people have generously given of their time and money to help us raise funds for the carers in Norfolk A comment from a carer echoes my feelings about the people with whom I share space here. Thank you to the trustees for all your help. It hurts to realise how very kind people are. I pray that this beautiful part of Norfolk in which I am privileged to live will survive for ever.

Maggie Secker has been with BBC Radio Norfolk since its inception in 1980 as a producer and presenter. In the early days she appeared regularly with Keith Skipper on his weekdays *Dinnertime Show*, but for many years has presented her chat-show, *Maggie's Brew*, on Sunday afternoons. In the series 'What Norfolk Means to Me', she wrote in the autumn 2006 edition of *The Merry Mawkin*:

Urge to go back to our roots

It seems we always have an urge to go back to our roots. I was born and brought up on a Norfolk farm in the days when a child could roam the countryside and take part in virtually all the farm activities.

To be out in the fields during the school holidays was bliss, although getting on the old bike for the ride to Attleborough station to catch the train to Thetford Girls' Grammar School at sugarbeet time wasn't quite so much fun.

The countryside lost its appeal during my teens. I had a great love of music but the big pop groups didn't come to Morley St Peter! It all happened in Norwich and other larger venues, which proved difficult when the last bus home was around 10 o'clock.

Teenagers didn't have cars like they do today to get around. I lived in Norwich for a short time in my twenties and discovered that the "Big City" had its own appeal.

There's much more to it than shops and crowds of people. Once I'd been told to look around me, appreciate the architecture, see the trees and shrubs which grace virtually every street,

Maggie Secker: 'One of the nicest parts of the world.'

I began to enjoy our county as a whole.

In 1978 I joined the BBC and Radio Norfolk when it came to our airwaves in 1980.

Since presenting *Maggie's Brew*, I've really started to learn about the county, home to so many talented people, many of them with a good old Norfolk twang.

I recall going on holiday with my new husband in the early 1970s and being made to feel about six inches tall by a rather 'posh' lady at our dining table in the hotel. "You're from Norfolk, aren't you? We have a lady at work with a funny little accent like you," she dared to say, looking down her nose at me.

Cor blast, bor, she wunt get away with that today, now would she! She'd be told firmly but fairly (to use a common phrase of a colleague) that 'I'm Norfolk and proud on ut'. We Norfolk people should never be ashamed of our Norfolk accents.

It hails from the fact that we were born in one of the nicest parts of the world. The coast, the Broads, wild countryside, pretty villages, wide open skies... it goes on and on...

And getting back to those roots. I now live up a rutty old loke with trailing brambles, wildlife a-plenty, and look forward to spending the rest of my days in the Norfolk countryside.

One regular contributor to *The Merry Mawkin* over the past ten years who has entertained our readers with some highly pertinent and humorous articles on dialect has managed to remain anonymous, sometimes using the pen-name **Outsider**, and on other occasions the

Norfolk colloquial name for a tadpole, **Polly Wiggle**. It is a shame that credit cannot be given publicly to the source of this prolific output, but I can say that one would not have to stray far from the FOND hierarchy to remove this literary mask!

Here's an early example of Outsider's thoughts expressed in Edition 4 of the *Mawkin* in the autumn of 2001:

Be proud of your accent

A couple of months ago I had the gift of a ticket to a *Press Gang show. For those who have not experienced this phenomenon, I should explain that it is an evening of Norfolk entertainment, songs, readings and humour with a generous dollop of local squit thrown in by our chairman for good measure.

In short, an education. One of the items was most unexpected and left the audience for a moment stunned before they appreciated its significance.

**Peter Whitbread, a regular member of the Press Gang and a classical actor of such standing that one could wonder how on earth he arrived in the middle of such rustic 'hempen homespuns' and performed a scene from *Romeo and Juliet* – in broad Norfolk!

Explaining that in Shakespeare's time female parts were played by men, he donned a gown and head-dress and proceeded to act the part of Juliet's nurse as she described her charge as a child – a Norfolk nurse – and why not?

Norfolk existed then as it does now. Indeed, one of Shakespeare's contemporaries, Robert Greene, also a playwright, came from Norwich. Is it beyond the bounds of possibility that Shakespeare heard Greene speak, and even liked the dialect? After all, Shakespeare even mentions a 'harnser' in one of his plays when referring to a heron. But my point is that the accent

** The Press Gang stood down in 2008 after 25 years of local entertaining for charity.*

*** Peter Whitbread was the speaker at a FOND-dew at Hoveton in 2003. Tragically, he died after a road accident in his home village of Briningham, near Holt, in 2004.*

was unexpected in such a setting. And it got me thinking about other occasions when an accent, perfectly delivered, has appeared by surprise.

I suppose the first time I recall was during a junior production of *The Mikado* in Warwickshire when, in the final denouement, the son of the Mikado appeared and announced: "But the heir apparent lives!" in a broad Birmingham accent. An additional surprise for the non-locals of the audience and lovely to hear – but it didn't quite match the kimono.

Another school production, this time *Androcles and the Lion*, performed in South Yorkshire. The centurion raised a laugh when he (she in this production) informed Androcles and his companions: "I'm reet sorry for thee, Christians, but tha'll have ter go t'lions" in an accent heard all over Sheffield. This time it was intended to, and did raise a laugh – but it didn't quite match the sandals and breastplate.

Also in Sheffield, while I was helping at a crèche looking after the youngsters of immigrant women who were being taught English, during a fairly lively game one simply beautiful little girl of Indian origin came out with a string of absolute back-street Sheffield in one of the purest accents I ever heard while living there. It stopped me dead – but it didn't quite match the fabulous miniature sari.

All memorable moments and all due to hearing local speech in its right locality – just unexpectedly. None of the exponents felt embarrassed or demeaned by use of the accent, it was pure instinct – just as it should be.

Be proud of your accent, wherever it comes from, whether it is absolutely pure or not (mine is a monstrous hybrid). You may have to explain some of the dialect occasionally to incomers, but maintaining all local speech is important and is part of the heritage of England.

Paul Barnes, former Anglia Television presenter and producer, has been host for some fifteen years of the acclaimed swing and jazz programme *Gold for Grownups*, broadcast on six BBC local radio stations on Saturdays throughout the Eastern Counties. Earlier in 2009 the programme was rescheduled from 6–9pm to 11pm–1am and renamed *The Late Paul Barnes*, adding BBC Radio Kent to its network.

For my final edition of *The Merry Mawkin*, No 24, winter, 2006, Paul Barnes contributed to the 'Norfolk by Adoption' series:

30 years: it looks as if I'm staying!

"Welcome to the graveyard of ambition." This was the late Paul Honeyman, head of features at Anglia TV, greeting me on my second day there in 1977. We were in the green room, where it was the custom for senior types to gather ostensibly to watch *About Anglia*, the regional news magazine, but in reality to sluice down drinks on the company.

Paul enlarged on his welcome by telling me that many an import before me had been happy to let the eiderdown of contentment settle around his shoulders as Norfolk absorbed him.

I knew a bit about the county. Having presented *Today* alongside John Timpson, the ultimate professional Norfolk man, how could I fail to be aware of the charms of the place? But I'd been aware of them long before, at the age of nine or ten, thanks to Arthur Ransome's *Coot Club* with its vivid picture of the Broads and the sheer pleasure of sailing quiet rivers. And that's another thing that Paul Honeyman told me: that I was bound to get myself a boat sometime. Everybody else seemed to.

Paul Barnes: 'Jealously fond of the place.'

There was another prior connection: railways. I'd been involved with the Association of Railway Preservation Societies, and in the mid-'sixties two rival factions were fighting each other for the stretch of line between Sheringham and Weybourne, a sweet remnant of the Midland and Great Northern Joint Railway.

The risk was that they would both fail and the line would be lost. The ARPS banged some heads together and it worked. Now the North Norfolk Railway is a flourishing affair. I used to visit often, staying on Kelling Heath and revelling the combined scent of pines, sea and steam, and I've still got my silver pass.

Later, in 1982, the scent of those pines formed part of a new experience, when I ran in the first Norfolk Marathon – 26 miles, 385 yards of seriously undulating road between Kelling and Norwich Cathedral – muttering Noel Coward's libellous line "very flat, Norfolk" through clenched teeth. I've been a runner ever since. Not the athletic type, I'm not built for it, but just to keep fit.

And the bonus is that running is slow enough for you to get a sense of place and a sense of the season. Try it at dawn. The other day I encountered a barn owl, silently seeking breakfast for its young, and successfully too. It passed me minutes later with a small rodent in its claws.

It's nearly 30 years since I came here, so it looks as though I'm staying. In fact, I've become so jealously fond of the place, wary of interlopers, that it may be time to reinstate a modest proposition that Keith Skipper and I discussed some years ago: a campaign to single the A11.

Will Martin was a journalist in his native Sheffield, also in the Seychelles and Dubai, before he and his wife Lynne opened a vegetarian café at Holt in the early 1990s. When I retired from the *Eastern Daily Press* in 1992, he replaced me as a sub-editor and joined our group of walkers on 'yomps' all over the county. Will, Lynne and I were among the eleven friends who in 2000, as related in Chapter 4, trekked 4,400 miles in a Land-Rover camping expedition in which we travelled far beyond the Arctic Circle through Norway, Sweden and Finland to the Russian border.

Will Martin: 'Norfolk enriched our lives.'

Will Martin is the author of two books on walking – *Pub Strolls in Norfolk* and *Adventurous Pub Walks in Norfolk*.

After redundancy in 2006, he was offered a post on the newspaper he had previously worked for in the Seychelles and returned there in the spring of 2008 on a two-year contract. In the summer of 2003, **Will Martin** wrote this piece in the *Mawkin's* 'Norfolk by Adoption' series:

You've made us feel at home

It took us a long time to get to Norfolk – up to five hours and a good 15 years, in fact.

After we started coming on family holidays and pondering on how pleasant it would be to live here, it was getting on for two decades before we finally made it, in the autumn of 1988.

And the five hours? That relates to those early expeditions from Sheffield in a car packed with camping gear and two hot, fractious kids in the back saying, "Are we nearly there yet?" every few miles. In front, the couple of hot, fractious adults knew full well we were not even close as the car crept through the mind-numbing Lincolnshire countryside in a convoy of lorries and caravans.

Those villages, before the A17 bypasses, formed a litany of despair. Leadenham, crawl up the hill; Swineshead, queue at the level crossing; Fosdyke, tailback at the bridge. Sutterton, Saracen's Head, Sutton Bridge... Even Clenchwarton, though nominally Norfolk, seemed only an extension of Lincolnshire, and if ever a place name summed up one's plight, it was that. We clenched and sincerely hoped the girls would clench until, at last,

King's Lynn and a more than welcome cup of tea.

Then, almost magically, things picked up. Even the regular torrential downpour at Knights Hill seemed no more than a dramatic introduction to a wholly different land. As we passed Fakenham and turned on to the minor road, the tall hedges on either side steered us unerringly to our destination – Wells-next-the-Sea.

Based at the Pinewoods campsite, tucked into its corner between channel and sea, it seemed to have everything we could wish for – expanses of sand and shallow pools for the children, lovely walks into the sunset towards Holkham, or eastwards past the quay with the marshes spread out below; an attractive time-warp sort of town where the holidaymakers quickly took on the unhurried style of the locals.

Norfolk enriched our lives enormously from the beginning. Like countless visits before and since, we loved the vast skyscapes with trees and churches set in bold relief and for me, in particular, the county's rich birdlife was a delight that has brought many hours of happiness.

We loved the vitality of the language with even more 'local' words in regular use than back home in South Yorkshire – 'squit' quickly passed into family usage and we marvelled at the inventiveness of words like bishy-barney-bee.

We came to know the people who spoke them and, realising their apparent aloofness was only a quirky, dry-humoured façade, we liked them too.

They – you – have made us feel at home.

In earlier *Mawkins*, FOND's treasurer Janet Woodhouse wrote a series on growing up at North Elmham in the 1940s and 1950s, and in the 2006 winter edition her mother, **Doris Yarham**, recalled working as a Norfolk landgirl in the same era:

Muck-spreading in the moonlight

By Doris Yarham

In the 'forties and 'fifties I worked on a mixed farm. I looked forward to the different seasons and varied jobs through the year.

One job I liked was on the drag-rake at harvest time. The horse I had to use was a chestnut called Prince. No one told me he had never been in a pair of shafts or a drag-rake and he had only been brought to the farm the night before. You can imagine what happened when I tripped the rake when it was full – luckily it was a 60-acre field!

I looked after quite a few laying hens as well as a small flock of geese for Christmas. The farm grew a few acres of carrots, and four women would spend the winter pulling them and bagging them. I also had to pull mangolds, top and tail them and grind them up – hard work.

With the wartime two-hour time difference, the working days were long and at harvest time we would come out of the fields in the moonlight.

To earn a little more, my husband and I, with two other men, would go muck-spreading in the moonlight!

Threshing was hard work. I always got the job of bagging the chaff and the wind was always blowing the wrong way!

Sometimes I would like to turn back the clock, even though it was hard work. There was the friendship with the men and women who worked on the farm and the satisfaction of a job well done. As the seasons come round, I still miss it, even though I am now well into my eighties.

In April 2002, a landmark BBC radio series was launched on Radio Norfolk exploring the historic and contemporary forces that have shaped our county. *A Sense of Place* consisted of six documentary programmes looking at people's personal connections to Norfolk and their experiences of living here. The producer, BBC Radio Norfolk's **Lyn McKinney**, wrote about it in the spring *Mawkin*:

A Sense of Place

I couldn't wait to start this series. When the six-month attachment for a producer for *A Sense of Place* was posted on the BBC Radio Norfolk notice board, I beat a path to the managing editor's door.

Though Sussex-born, I've come to regard Norfolk as home, after 26 years living and raising a family here. So the production of six radio documentaries as part of a national BBC landmark project for transmission in the spring has been a labour of love.

My first action was to talk to people throughout the county who might give me an overview of how Norfolk ticks. There would be a programme which looked at the Norfolk character – its language, its humour and its image, which is where Keith Skipper and friends have been invaluable. One of Norfolk's best-known ambassadors, Stephen Fry, agreed to narrate that one, to my delight, and the Lord Lieutenant, Sir Timothy Colman – also a great supporter of FOND – is included in that programme.

Lyn McKinney: 'Wonderful people.'

Then, because so many people like me have moved to Norfolk and stayed, I wondered what sort of impression Norfolk gives to newcomers, not just from London or other parts of the UK, but from other countries. A second programme idea was born.

Then David Clayton, my managing editor, said: "Wouldn't it be amazing if we could capture the real sounds of the county in glorious stereo?" Hence the presence of the *Norfolk Soundtrack* programme through 24 hours, beginning with the dawn chorus and as much of Norfolk life as I could manage. Then a programme entitled *Postcards from the Edge*, celebrating the lives of those who live and work on the very rim of the county, from Blakeney Point to Hopton, Santon Downham and the Walpoles.

It occurred to me that young people should have their say, so I asked a group of students to keep audio diaries of the places in which they live. They came up trumps with some really refreshing thoughts. Finally, a sixth programme, working title *Norwich – a Fine City?* looks at the changing face of Norwich.

It 's been a delight and a privilege to make these programmes. I've met some wonderful people and learned so much about the county.

And in the 2002 summer/autumn edition, **Lyn McKinney** was also the contributor in the 'Norfolk by Adoption' series:

Among my dearest friends

Three months after I moved to south Norfolk from London in 1975 I seemed no further forward in getting to know neighbours and mentioned the fact to someone I had got to know. "Don't you worry," she said. "They know all about you."

It's part of the Norfolk character, I've now come to realise, and admire, to stand back a little and observe, before leaping in… and now, nearly 30 years later, I count many Norfolk people among my dearest friends. People you can rely on in a crisis... And in the end, isn't that what counts?

But Norfolk took a bit of getting used to. For a start, I had to slow down when out walking, because I'd become accustomed to striding through crowded tube stations in London, elbows at the ready. I had to get used to being left in the dark for hours, when high winds would cause huge tree branches to clash with electricity wires, and cut the power. But the biggest difference was the space. Lots of lovely elbow room. We swapped our pocket handkerchief garden in London for over two acres in Norfolk... And all our London friends who came for the weekend were expected to put in time in the vegetable patch.

Slowly, over the years, rather tenuous roots put down in Sussex during a childhood spent moving from place to place, were replaced by more permanent ones in Norfolk, in a clay-lump cottage 20 minutes from the centre of Norwich. Two daughters and a dog completed the family. I can't pretend my relationship with Norfolk would have been the same if I hadn't begun working for Radio Norfolk back in 1981.

Over the last 20 odd years I've had the privilege of meeting some fascinating and wonderful people, whether it's been out reporting in the county, or meeting guests here at our Norfolk Tower home. Though the Norfolk landscape is diverse, and often unexpectedly beautiful, in the end it is the people that make a place.

I wasn't born here, and therefore can't claim to be a Norfolk person, but I hope I can now say I qualify by adoption. All this from a hardened old journalist – is this Norfolk getting to me?

Louise Priest began her broadcasting career at BBC Radio Norfolk as a young and enthusiastic reporter and within two years she had become a producer and presented the afternoon show. After four years, a marriage and family commitments took her off to Essex. Later she rejoined Radio Norfolk to present the early morning *Today in Norfolk.* Currently, she presents the early Sunday morning programme. In the 2003 spring edition of *The Merry Mawkin*, Louise wrote in the 'Norfolk by Adoption' series:

Truly settled in unique county

Strange as it may seem, the first thing that really struck me about Norfolk was just how lovely the roundabouts were as I travelled into Norwich.

There seemed to be an endless procession of beautifully manicured flowering beds which certainly put me in good spirits as I cautiously made my way to Radio Norfolk for the first time.

Louise Priest: 'I've loved the county from that first day.'

Until that day I knew where Norfolk was but had only heard stories from the lucky people of the Midlands (I come from Leicestershire) who came here to stay or had a home here. I wish I'd been introduced sooner... All those lost years!

I've loved the county from that first day, in the early 1980s, all for the obvious reasons: the glorious countryside, beaches and friendly people. Although there were one or two who were a little suspicious of me at first – another incomer, eh?

I was lucky enough to see quite a lot of Norfolk through my job, reporting for both BBC Radio Norfolk and *Look East* and soon began to feel this really was home.

The nearby coast was a big draw, too, having lived throughout my childhood in the middle of the country, the idea of being near the sea seemed particularly attractive. At last, half an hour in the car and I'd be paddling.

In subsequent years, the draw of the sea has remained just as great (the wilder the better in north Norfolk!). I remember one day I visited my in-laws at West Runton. I had a sudden urge to go to the beach; the fact it was nearly dark and the middle of the winter was neither here nor there!

I am proud to say I've done a lot more than just dip my toe in the North Sea over the years. We have spent many a happy day on the beach at Gorleston being proper 'grackles' (tourists to you and me). A picnic ball game and, of course, a swim, not to mention the frothy coffee from the nearby café – bliss!

A decade later we had to part from Norfolk due to my husband's job, but as soon as the chance came up, we were back. We had two children by then and felt how lovely it would be for them to grow up here.

Having been back now for more than seven years, we feel truly settled and, dare I say, the odd Norfolk pronunciation slips out, even on the air. Does that mean I'm a true native?

Our pal Keith Skipper pops in to the programme once a month to remind us of the wealth of stories, history and characters that make this county unique. I'm happy to say I can understand most of what he's going on about too!

Since Ashley Gray became editor of *The Merry Mawkin* in 2007, a regular contributor has been his fellow Wymondhamian and FOND member, **Tina Chamberlain**, author of two books of poems – *I Sit Here Thinkun* and *Um Stilla Thinkun*. From the latter, on the next page, is a poetic memory of her childhood:

Tina Chamberlain and her books: I Sit Here Thinkun and Um Stilla Thinkun.

My Norfolk Upbringun

A little country bungalow
Is where I was born 'n' raised.
Mum 'n' Dad had nine a us,
They were the good ole days.

Um Tina, um the youngest.
I don't do girlie things like cook,
I'd rather be out fishun,
Mum said I orta bin a blook.

I learnt ta drive a tractor,
I loved thut every bit,
I'd pull ma father on the trailer
While he forked orf the chicken muck.

We grew our cabbages 'n' spuds
An' carrots by the score.
I loved the tearst a them.
They just aren't the searme na more.

Our ole tin bath ud hang outside
An' Fridays arter nosh
We'd hev thut ole bath indoors
An' all on us hed a wash.

Mum used ta git ma clothes
From the Army 'n' Navy store.
You don't see gals at school
Dressed as soldiers anymore.

You know I love ta reminisce.
Our Mum 'n' Dad were funny.
They give us many laughs 'n' love,
Ya can't buy thut wi' money.

David Whiteley wrote in *The Merry Mawkin's* 'Norfolk by Adoption' series in the summer edition of 2005:

> My name's David Whiteley, I'm 28 years old and I live in Norfolk. I present the BBC One current affairs programme *Inside Out* and I'm currently working on my eighth series. I'm also a producer and director on the programme.
>
> I first got into broadcasting ten years ago, getting my first job in the newsroom of my local commercial radio station in my native Essex. It was a baptism of fire, being the new boy, and a trainee journalist. They take no prisoners in hectic newsrooms.
>
> I became a newsreader at the station and then was lucky enough to land a job at the BBC local radio station. After three-and-a-half happy years (getting up at 4am for the breakfast shift.... so not THAT happy), I moved into TV. And that's how I ended up here, an Essex boy in Norfolk.

You name the beach, I've surfed it!

> I started reporting for BBC *Look East* and this was a great vehicle to get me around the county. Coming from Essex, one thing you don't realise is just how much of the sky you DON'T see!! That is until you get up the A140 and into Norfolk. Fantastic! It really is a great place, full of great people.
>
> I didn't think there were any genuinely friendly people left, until you get to Norfolk. Ok, you get the point, you're all lovely!
>
> When I was offered the job presenting *Inside Out*, it took me at least one second to think about it! And that's when the real fun began and Norfolk's coastline took me to the edge!

PICTURE: SIMON BUCK PHOTOGRAPHY

David Whiteley: 'Here feels like home.'

We made a film about surfing the East Coast and a year later I haven't stopped surfing. Cromer, Mundesley, Bacton, you name the beach, I've surfed it. In all weathers, and in deepest winter too!

I think one of my lasting memories was sharing the surf at Bacton with a rather over-curious seal, on January 3 this year! The friendly locals say, "You're brave!" to which I reply, "No, just stupid!"

I have to say that the sea is where I feel most at home. Having been brought up a Sea Scout in Essex, it's very natural to me. Either in it or on it, that's home.

I fell in love with north Norfolk the moment I went, and I get up there even when the surf's flat! I have friends who live in Wells and we'll strike out from there to Sheringham, Blakeney, all the paces we know so well.

Every year I get asked to host the Wells Harbour Day... always great. I'm almost part of the furniture there now. A few glasses of cider and my commentary gets more and more risqué. Last year the poor old Sheringham Shanty Men had no choice when me and the harbour master joined in for the finale! I may not be invited back this year!

Even though Essex is my birthplace, having been in Norfolk four years, here feels like home. And there's nothing better than surfing all day and getting home to Thorpe St Andrew on the river for a pint! Cheers, Norfolk!

Charles Roberts, former *Eastern Daily Press* literary and arts editor, prizewinning theatre critic, author, actor, lecturer and conservationist, came to Norfolk planning to stay six months. Three decades later he was still here and he wrote this article for *The Merry Mawkin* in the 'Norfolk by Adoption' series for the spring edition in 2002.

For many years an ardent Francophile, it came as no surprise to *EDP* friends and colleagues like myself when Charles announced that he planned to emigrate to France.

It is now six years since Charles left England, but he has kept in touch ever since through his weekly Tuesday column, Letter from France, in the *EDP*, finally retiring in August, 2009.

Adopted by Norfolk!

It all began by purest chance. I'd been working abroad for three years, in baking hot Kuwait and, what with the heat and the equally simmering politics, I decided three years was enough.

So I returned to England, to my native village in north Staffordshire, and set about searching for another overseas job. Three months on, nothing had materialised. "Come on, Roberts," nagged A Little Voice in the back of my head, "get something temporary to keep you going."

Charles Roberts: 'Rural richness.'

That 'something temporary' was a move to Norfolk – "Nice place," observed Little Voice approvingly. "We had a Broads holiday here when you were a teenager." Which is how I landed a role on the *Eastern Daily Press* with the absolute intention that this should be a six-month stop gap!

The music critic and arts man at that time was a marvellous character named George Usher, who had a passion for classical music and a colourful vocabulary to make a soldier blanch. Alas, he also lived on cigarettes. A year after arrival, dear old George passed on – and I inherited his mantle, and was invested with the title of Literary and Arts Editor.

I stayed in that post for 28 years – so much for a six-month stop gap! I'd been fairly warned. I remember at George's memorial service at St Peter Mancroft in Norwich, the then vicar (later Bishop of Peterborough) Bill Westwood, another unforgettably splendid character, gave an oration which vividly caught the image of both George, and of the county he loved.

Norfolk, said Bill, was a place which, imperceptibly, sank gentle claws into you, and claimed you for its own. How true. I came to love, as much as any native, the gently rolling countryside, in all its rich variety from Brecks to coast and all its rural richness in between. But something else attracted my passion.

Since the age of 15 or 16, back in my native county, I'd been fascinated by medieval churches, and all they had to show us in history, architecture, art and belief. With my best pal (who became a priest in God's good time) I biked untold miles to pick out the best churches where we set down our observations in careful notebooks, and recorded them on photo film.

So when I'd settled into Norfolk and really begun to explore, I soon realised that in terms of fine medieval houses of God, I'd stumbled on a treasury. Since then, I've written books on the subject, and for the past 12 years taken small groups of people – who have become a company of friends – on 'church crawls' around the county, sharing my enthusiasm, and passing on what limited knowledge I have.

Of course the arts, with theatre and opera in the forefront, have deeply occupied me too, not just as a job, but as something to which I have a real commitment, and to which I owe eternal gratitude for giving me so much pleasure and inspiration. Sentiments, indeed, which attach with equal affection to this very special county in which we live.

Doon't lose the Dodman

By Mike Coley

What happened to the dodman?
And bishy-barney-bees?
An' even old King Harry
A'sittin' in the trees?

Well, truth is, my old bewty,
Outsiders wi' big snouts
Hev cum along an' chearnged their names,
But they're still here abouts.

We'll oll'us hev the Frenchman
A'skootn'n crorst the smeath,
Then hedgy Betts a'chirp'n
An' rannies with sharp teeth.

An' folks'll swat at wapsies
An' call out, "Look up, bor,"
Then larf and say "Don't worry
Thass just a mitchamador"

Now if yew goo a'fishun',
At least yew orta try,
An' don't kick up a dullar
Dew yew'll meark the harnser fly.

Corse catch'n fish's one thing
But clean'n orf the scales
'll meark yew dream'a Stewkey Blues
Wot yew collect in pails.

And inland on the medder
When look'n arter stock
Yew wanta wotch the canker weed
Or yew mite get a shock.

Though if yew're got a dicky
He'll never teark much harm,
He'll even eat the thistles
Wot grow about the farm.

An' when yew goo a'trosh'n,
Teark yew a grut big stick,
Lest yew catch Sally napp'n
Though yew'll hatta be right quick.

So there y'ar tergether,
Thass just a little peep
At friends wot live about us
Whose names we wanta keep.

We've oll'us dun things different
So less jus' carry on,
Or names we've loved,
I guarantee, forever will be gone.

Doon't yew let'ut happen,
tergether!

First published in The Merry Mawkin, in Edition 10, summer 2003.

About the author

ROBIN LIMMER was born at Broome on the Norfolk side of the River Waveney and was educated on the Suffolk side at Bungay Grammar School. He entered journalism in 1949 as a trainee reporter on the *Norfolk Chronicle* at Fakenham. Six months later he was appointed district reporter at North Walsham.

After two years' National Service in the RAF he returned to the *Norfolk Chronicle* as chief reporter and deputy editor. In 1955 he joined the *Eastern Daily Press* as district reporter at Sheringham. In 1958 he moved to head office in Norwich to become an *EDP* sub-editor, retiring in 1992. He was secretary of the company's sailing club for 18 years.

Since 1992 he has been a team editor and music editor with the *Three Rivers Talking Newsaper for the Blind* in the Bungay, Beccles, Loddon and Halesworth areas. He was editor of FOND's newsletter, *The Merry Mawkin*, from 2001–2004 and during 2006.

He is married to Shelagh, has two sons, four grandchildren and five great-grandchildren, and lives at Denton, near Harleston.

Bibliography

Confessions of a Norfolk Squit Merchant, by Keith Skipper. Halsgrove, 2008.

How to Survive in Norfolk, by Keith Skipper. Halsgrove, 2007.

The Boy John Letters, by Sidney Grapes: A Fresh Delivery from Keith Skipper. Mousehold Press, 2003.

Hev Yew Gotta Loight, Boy? by Keith Skipper. Countryside Books, 2001.

Skipper's Byways, by Keith Skipper. *Eastern Daily Press*, 1998.

Larn Yarself Norfolk, by Keith Skipper. Nostalgia Publications, 1996.

The Norfolk Companion, by Keith Skipper. Jim Baldwin Publishing, Fakenham, 1994.

The Norfolk Connection, by Keith Skipper. Poppyland Publishing, 1991.

The Norfolk Dialect, by Peter Trudgill. Poppyland Publishing, 2003.

Sociolinguistic Variation and Change, by Peter Trudgill. Edinburgh University Press.

The Place of Norfolk Among English Dialects, by Peter Trudgill. From *The Merry Mawkin*, 2001.

Woordenboek der Nederlandsche Taal, (Dictionary of the Dutch Language).

Van Dale's Modern Dutch Dictionary.

The Oxford English Dictionary.

Dictionary of American Regional English (DARE).

Forby's Vocabulary of East Anglia. 1830.

No Going Back, by Martin Kirby. Time Warner Paperbacks, 2003.

Mighta Bin Wuss: Tales of the Boy Jimma, by Tony Clarke. Nostalgia Publications, 1998.

Broad Norfolk, by Jonathan Mardle. Wensum Books, 1973.

Ted Ellis's Countryside Reflections, by Ted Ellis. Phyllis Ellis, 2001.

Prewd and Prejudice: A Norfolk Exile, by Chris Sugden and Sid Kipper. Mousehold Press,1994.

The Norfolk Dialect: Guides to Reading and Research, by Ron Fiske. From *The Merry Mawkin*, 2006.

Beccles Talk 2001: A Speech Odyssey, by Anne Frith, Dorothy Smith and Anne Bauers.

Talking for Britain: A Journey Through the Nation's Dialects, by Simon Elmes. Penguin.

English Dialect Grammar and English Dialect Dictionary, by Dr Joseph Wright. 1904.

EDP Country Walks (series: seventh, 2009), by Charles and Joy Boldero. *Eastern Daily Press.*

The Norfolk Walker's Book, by Bruce Robinson. Elmstead Publications, 1998.

Adventurous Pub Walks in Norfolk, by Will Martin. Countryside Books, 2003.

Pub Strolls in Norfolk, by Will Martin. Countryside Books, 2001.

Albie's Poems: Reflection of a Norfolk Lad, by Ashley Gray. Geo R Reeve Ltd, 2007.

Albie's Thoughts: A Poetic Journey Through Bygone Seasons, by Ashley Gray. Geo R Reeve Ltd, 2007.

I Sit Here Thinkun: Poems of Days Gone, by Tina Chamberlain. 2006.

Um Stilla Thinkun: More poems of my past, by Tina Chamberlain. 2007.

LOCAL TITLES PUBLISHED BY JOHN NICKALLS PUBLICATIONS

A Garland of Waveney Valley Tales – A compilation of illustrated tales from Suffolk of yesteryear.

A Level Country – Sketches of its Fenland folk and history.

A Pharmacist's Tale – The joys and delights encountered preserving pharmacy history.

A Shepherd and his Flock – Fifty years with Suffolk sheep.

Curiosities of Norfolk – A county guide to the unusual.

Curiosities of Suffolk – A county guide to the unusual.

Great Ouse Country – Sketches of its riverside folk and history from source to mouth.

Great Yarmouth & Gorleston: Then and Now – A Pictorial tour in old postcards and modern-day photographs.

Harwich, Dovercourt & Parkeston, Vol 3 A further selection of old picture postcards.

Harwich, Dovercourt & Parkeston: Then and Now – Comparing the aura of yesterday with its modern counterpart.

In and Around Norwich, Then and Now – A further look at Norwich and district.

Melton Constable, Briston & District, Book 1 – A portrait in old picture postcards.

Melton Constable, Briston & District, Book 2 – A further portrait in old picture postcards.

Nature Trails in Northamptonshire – A series of illustrated walks.

Newmarket, Town and Turf – A pictorial tour.

North Norfolk – A portrait in old picture postcards.

North Norfolk: The Heritage Coast – Timeless scenes captured by the lens.

Norwich: Then and Now – A look at the city through old postcards and modern photographs.

Norwich: Then and Now – A third selection of old picture postcards.

Robber Barons and Fighting Bishops – The Norman influence in East Anglia.

Shires, Sales and Pigs – The story of an Ely family of Auctioneers. George Comins, 1856–1997.

Suffolk's Lifeboats – A portrait in postcards and photographs.

S'Wonderful – A symphony of musical memories.

'Smarvellous – More musical memories.

Tipple & Teashop Rambles in Northamptonshire – A series of illustrated walks.

Walks in the Wilds of Cambridgeshire – A series of illustrated walks.

Wicken: a Fen Village – A third selection of old pictures.